MANUALS OF ELEMENTARY SCIENCE.

BOTANY.

BY

PROFESSOR BENTLEY,

Honorary Fellow of King's College, London; Honorary Member of the
Pharmaceutical Society of Great Britain; Honorary Member of the
American Pharmaceutical Association, &c., &c. Author of
"Manual of Botany," &c., &c.

PUBLISHED UNDER THE DIRECTION OF
THE COMMITTEE OF GENERAL LITERATURE AND EDUCATION
APPOINTED BY THE SOCIETY FOR PROMOTING
CHRISTIAN KNOWLEDGE.

LONDON:

SOCIETY FOR PROMOTING CHRISTIAN KNOWLEDGE.
SOLD AT THE DEPOSITORIES:
77, GREAT QUEEN STREET, LINCOLN'S INN FIELDS
4, ROYAL EXCHANGE; 48, PICCADILLY;
AND BY ALL BOOKSELLERS.

NEW YORK: POTT, YOUNG & CO.

1875.

191. k. 133

PREFACE.

THIS little book on Botany has been prepared with the intention of supplying young boys and girls with a simple introduction to the study of plants. It is written in as plain language as possible; but when we consider the almost infinite varieties of form and arrangement which the different parts of plants assume, and the absolute necessity of giving a name to each variation, in order that they may be properly described and recognised, it is clear that in a book on botany, however elementary, the use of certain technical terms is essential, and could not therefore be avoided in the present work. But we have endeavoured to express their meaning in such a way as to be quite intelligible to any boy or girl beyond the age of twelve years, who has even received but a moderately good education.

This elementary work has been limited to a description of the forms and structure of the various parts of plants; their study must necessarily precede all other departments of botany, and form the foundation to a knowledge of the names, arrangement, properties, and uses of plants, as also of the laws which regulate their life. The consideration of these latter departments we leave for the present, but with the hope of being able to treat of them hereafter in a second elementary book on botany. As now designed, the present work is especially calculated to form a simple introduction to the use of the Rev. C. A. Johns' "Flowers of the Field," already published by the Society for Promoting

Christian Knowledge, and the author's "Manual of Botany."

No study is better calculated than that of plants to sharpen the powers of observation in the minds of youth, and to lead to methodical habits and accurate discrimination. There is, moreover, nothing repulsive in plants, but their beauty at once attracts attention; and as they may be found everywhere and at all seasons of the year, their study will afford an endless source of interest, and add increasing pleasure to our daily walks.

It seems impossible that any one with a properly regulated mind could contemplate the beautiful forms and arrangements of the different parts of plants, the wonderful ways in which they adapt themselves to the conditions under which they are placed, and their influence in nature, without having his thoughts elevated from these manifest evidences of God's work to Him who designed them, and without being satisfied to rest in faith, and in the full belief that He who has thus clothed the plants of the field will never be unmindful of him—His noblest work—a being endowed with a soul, and adapted for a higher and happier existence hereafter.

In conclusion, the author cannot but very strongly urge upon those who have any influence in directing the teaching of the young, that a study possessing so many advantages as botany, should form a branch of elementary education in all schools.

LONDON, *May*, 1875.

CONTENTS.

ELEMENTARY BOTANY.

GENERAL INTRODUCTION.

The study of the various bodies which are placed on the surface of the earth, or which combine to form its substance, constitutes what is called Natural History. These different substances are at once readily arranged in three great divisions, which are respectively characterised as the *Animal*, *Vegetable*, and *Mineral Kingdoms;* and as those comprised in .the two former are living bodies, they are also termed *Organic*, while those of the latter division, not being endowed with life, are called *Inorganic*. Botany is the science which treats of the lower members of the Organic world, termed Plants or Vegetables; and it embraces the study of everything which has reference to them, whether in a living or fossil state. Thus, it investigates their forms and structure; the laws which regulate their life and distribution at the present time, and in past ages of the world's history; and also includes their arrangement and classification, and a description of their properties and uses. In this elementary work we only propose to treat very briefly, and in the simplest possible language, of the forms and structure of plants and their parts or organs, leaving for another volume their classification, properties, and uses. The department of botany now to be treated of is technically called Organography, and comprises the study of the outward forms and internal structure of plants and their various parts or organs.

Organography, or, as its name implies, that department of botany which relates to the description of the organs of plants, is again subdivided into Morphology, or that part which has reference to their outward forms; and Structural Botany, which includes all that relates to their internal structure.

We shall commence with Morphology, as this part of our subject will be best understood by those who are commencing the study of botany.

ORGANOGRAPHY; OR DESCRIPTION OF THE
ORGANS OF PLANTS.

—◆—

PART I.

MORPHOLOGY OF PLANTS; OR MORPHOLOGICAL BOTANY.

CHAPTER I.

INTRODUCTORY.

BEFORE proceeding to describe more in detail the various organs of plants in their proper order, we will, in this introductory chapter, first trace their development from the rudimentary state in which they exist in the seed; then proceed to their general description; and conclude with a sketch of the characters of the principal subdivisions of plants.

We commence with a general description of the seed. If we take an Almond and blanch it, as it is commonly called, we find that this seed is composed of two parts—a brownish skin or seed-coat, which we have removed in blanching, and a large white fleshy mass situated within this, to which the name of embryo has been given. This embryo is the most important part of the seed, as it contains in itself all the fundamental organs of the future plant in a rudimentary state, and also a portion designed for their nourishment in the early stage of their growth—that is, before they are sufficiently developed to become independent and support themselves. The constituent parts of the embryo of the Almond are as follows :—1st. Two fleshy lobes, of equal size and shape (fig. 1, *c d*), which form by far the greater portion of the seed, and which may be readily separated from each other. To these lobes the name of *seed-leaves* or *cotyledons* has been given ; they are also called nursing leaves, because they are reservoirs of nutriment for the parts of the rudimentary plant in the early stage of their growth. 2nd. Between these lobes at their lower part, and connecting them together, we find a small central axis with two opposite extremities, the lower rounded, *r*, called the *radicle*, and the upper extremity, *g*, which is terminated by two or more rudimentary leaves, is termed the *plumule* or *gemmule*.

Fig. 1.	Fig. 2.	Fig. 3.

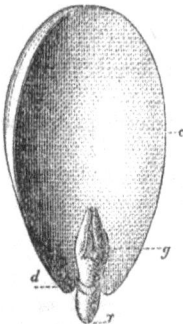 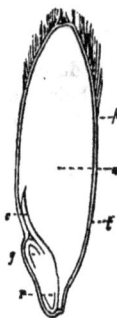 

Fig. 1.—Embryo of the Almond from which one of the cotyledons has been removed: *c*, cotyledon which has been left; *d*, scar left by the removal of the other cotyledon; *g*, plumule; *r*, radicle. Fig. 2.—Vertical section of the fruit of the Oat; *p*, pericarp; *t*, integuments or seed-coats; *a*, albumen ; *c*, cotyledon ; *g*, plumule; *r*, radicle. Fig. 3.—Seed after germination : *c c*, cotyledons ; *l*, leaves; *s*, stem ; *r*, root.

The embryo of all seeds is necessarily composed of a radicle, plumule, and cotyledonary body; but the latter is not always divisible into two parts—thus in the Oat it is undivided (fig. 2, c). And from this difference in the structure of the embryo we divide flowering plants—that is, those that are reproduced by seeds—into two great classes, which are technically termed Dicotyledons (*two cotyledons*) (figs. 1 and 3, c), and Monocotyledons (*one cotyledon*) (fig. 2, c). All other plants, such as Ferns, Mosses, and Sea-weeds, have no true flowers or seeds, and have, therefore, no cotyledons, and accordingly form a class by themselves called Acotyledons (*without cotyledons*). These are the three great divisions of plants.

When a seed is placed under favourable conditions its embryo (fig. 3) developes in a downward direction from the radicle, while the upper part grows upwards, carrying the plumule with it, and at the same time the cotyledonary portion becomes developed, and forms the first leafy organs. This development of the embryo constitutes what is called the process of germination. In this way we have formed a central axis, which grows in two opposite directions, the lower part of which is called the *descending axis* or *root*, r, and the upper, the *ascending axis* or *stem*, s. Upon this stem all the future organs of a plant are placed; those which directly succeed the cotyledons, c c, constitute the first true leaves, l, of the plant, and all which succeed these leaves, such as the parts of the flower, are simply modifications of those organs which have preceded them, designed for special purposes. Hence the three organs, namely, root, stem, and leaves, which originally exist in a rudimentary state in the embryo, are termed the *fundamental organs of the plant*, or from the fact of their having for their object the nutrition and development of the plant to which they belong; they are also called *organs of nutrition* or *vegetation;* while the parts of the flower having assigned to them the office of reproducing the plant by the formation of seeds, are termed *organs of reproduction.*

In like manner we have in Ferns, and other flowerless

plants, two distinct series of organs—one for nutrition, and another for reproduction. Hence in describing the organs of all plants we arrange them in two divisions, as follows:—1. *Organs of Nutrition;* and 2. *Organs of Reproduction.* It is now necessary, before describing these several organs more in detail, that we should briefly define them, and explain the terms by which their principal modifications are described.

1. ORGANS OF NUTRITION.—*a. The Root.*—The root (fig. 3, *r*) is that part of a plant which at its first development in the embryo takes a direction opposite to the stem, avoiding the light and air, and therefore termed the descending axis, and fixing the plant to the soil or to the substance upon which it grows, or floating in the water when the plant is placed upon the surface of that medium.

b. The Stem.—The stem (fig. 3, *s*) is that organ which at its first development passes upwards, seeking

Fig. 4.

the light and air, and hence termed the ascending axis, and bearing on its surface leaves, *l*, and other leafy appendages. In the angle formed by the junction of the upper surface of the leaf with the stem, a little more or less conical body called a *leaf-bud* (fig. 4, *b*) is commonly placed. It is in the presence of leaves and leaf-buds that we find the essential characters of a stem, as both these parts are absent in a root. The larger divisions of a

Fig 4.—Portion of a branch with leaf *l*, and bud *b*.

stem are called *branches*, and the small ramifications *twigs*.

c. The Leaf.—The leaf is commonly a more or less flattened expansion of the stem or branch (fig. 4, *l*), and the point from which it arises is called a *node*. The most highly developed leaves consist of three parts, namely, of an expanded portion, which is generally more or less flattened (fig. 6, *l*), called the *lamina* or *blade;* of a narrower part, by which this blade is connected with the stem, termed the *petiole* or *leaf-stalk*, *p;* and of a third portion at the base of the leaf, which exists in the form of a sheath surrounding the stem (fig. 5, *d*), or as two little leaf-like appendages on each side, termed *stipules* (fig. 6, *s s*). These three parts are not, however, necessarily present in all leaves, one or even two may be absent; the blade is the part more commonly found, and which, in ordinary language, is generally called the leaf.

Fig. 5.

Fig. 5.—Leaf and piece of the stem of the Water-pepper: *l*, lamina; *p*, petiole; *d*, sheath. Fig. 6.—Leaf and portion of a branch of a species of Willow: *br*, branch; *l*, lamina; *p*, petiole; *s s*, stipules.

2. ORGANS OF REPRODUCTION.—*a. The Flower-Stalk* or *Peduncle.*—The stalk upon which one or more flowers is placed is called the *floral axis* or *peduncle* (fig. 7, *p*); and if this branches, each stalk bearing a flower is termed a pedicel, *ped.* This axis frequently bears upon its surface, below the flowers, *f*, properly so called, other leafy organs, which are called *bracts* or *floral leaves, b.* These bracts may either be green, and in other respects

resemble the ordinary leaves of the stem or branch, or they may differ from such leaves in colour and other peculiarities. The arrangement of the flowers upon the floral axis is termed the *inflorescence*.

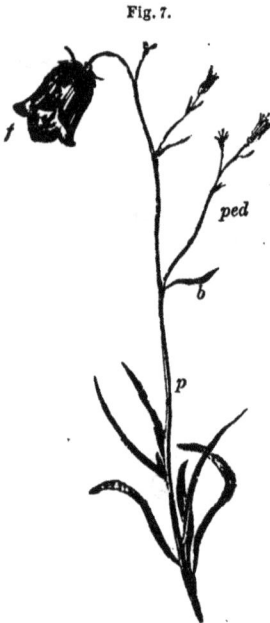

Fig. 7.

b. The Flower.—A flower (fig. 8) in its most complete state of development consists of four distinct series of organs, that is, of two internal or essential organs of reproduction, *o* and *st*, and two external enveloping organs which are especially designed for their protection (fig. 8, *cc* and *pp*), and which are called the *floral envelopes*. The essential organs are termed the *andrœcium* and *gynœcium*, and the enveloping organs *calyx* and *corolla*, and the part of the axis upon which these parts are placed is called the *thalamus, t*. These four series of organs forming the flower are arranged as four circles

Fig. 7.—The Harebell: *p*, peduncle; *ped*, pedicel; *b*, bract; *f*, flower.

upon the thalamus in the following order, from without inwards:—

1. Calyx. 2. Corolla. 3. Andrœcium. 4. Gynœcium.

The *Calyx* (fig. 8, *c c*) is the circle (or whorl, as it is commonly called) of leafy organs forming the outer envelope of the flower. Its parts are called *sepals*, and these are generally of a green colour, like the ordinary leaves of the plant, to which in other respects they have commonly a great resemblance.

The *Corolla* is the second whorl or circle of leafy organs situated within the calyx, and forming the inner envelope of the flower (fig. 8, *p p*). Its parts, which are

Fig. 8.   Fig. 9.

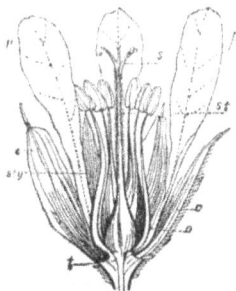 

Fig. 8.—Section of the flower of Herb-Robert, a species of Geranium : *c c*, calyx ; *p p*, petals; *st*, stamens ; *o*, gynœcium or pistil, composed of ovary *o*, style *sty*, and stigmas *s* ; *t*, thalamus. Fig. 9.—Flower of Goosefoot.

called *petals*, are commonly decorated with the richest · colours, or some other colour than green, by which peculiarity, and by their more delicate nature, they may be usually known from the sepals. In such flowers as the Tulip, Crocus, and more generally in monocotyledonous plants, the two floral envelopes resemble each other in being commonly both *coloured* or *petaloid* in their nature. In this case, instead of using the terms calyx and corolla, as previously defined, we speak of the two floral envelopes collectively under the name of *perianth*.

The floral envelopes are also called the *non-essential* organs of the flower, because their presence is not absolutely necessary for the production of the seed. Sometimes one floral envelope only is present, as in the Goosefoot (fig. 9); this is then properly regarded as the calyx, whatever be its colour or other peculiarity, and the flower is described as *apetalous*. At other times, as in the Willow and Ash (fig. 10), both floral envelopes are absent, when the flower is termed *naked*.

Fig. 10.　　　　Fig. 11.　　　　Fig. 12.

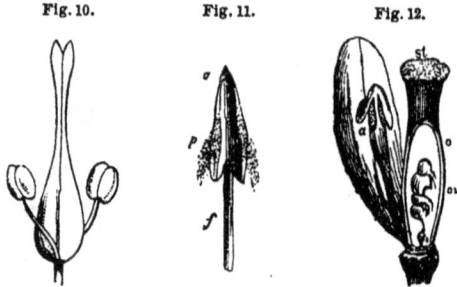

Fig. 10.—Flower of the common Ash.　Fig. 11.—A stamen of the Wallflower: *f*, filament; *a*, anther; *p*, pollen.　Fig. 12.—Vertical section of the ovary of the Barberry: *o*, ovary; *ov*, ovules attached to a projection called the placenta; *st*, stigma; *a*, anther.

The *Andrœcium* is situated inside the corolla, and receives its name from constituting the male system of flowering plants. It consists of one or more parts called stamens (fig. 8, *st*), each of which is essentially composed of a bag or case called the *anther* (fig. 11, *a*), which contains in its interior a powdery-looking substance called the *pollen, p;* and commonly also of a little stalk upon which the anther is placed, termed the *filament, f.*

The *Gynæcium*, or *Pistil* as it is also called, receives its name from its constituting the female system of flowering plants. It is situated in the centre of the flower, and is composed of one or more parts called *carpels* (figs. 8 and 12). Each carpel consists of a hollow inferior portion, called the *ovary* (fig. 12, *o*), in which are placed one or more little bodies called *ovules, ov,* which ultimately, by impregnation from the pollen, become the *seeds;* of a *stigma* or space of variable size, and usually distinguished by its loose viscid tissue, which is either placed immediately on the top of the ovary, as in the Barberry (fig. 12, *st*), or it is situated on a stalk-like portion prolonged from the ovary, as in the Geranium (fig. 8, *sty*), called the *style*.

The stamens and carpels are called essential organs, because the presence of both is absolutely necessary for the formation of perfect seed. It does not, however, always happen that a flower possesses both these organs —that is, is *bisexual*; one may be absent, as in the Willow and Sedge, when the flower is said to be *uni-sexual*, and it is further described as *staminate* or *male* (fig. 70), and *pistillate*, *carpellary*, or *female* (fig. 71), according as it contains one or the other of these organs.

c. The Fruit and Seed.—At a certain period, which varies in different flowers, the anther opens and dis-charges its pollen upon the stigma, by which the pistil is fertilised, and immediately afterwards important changes take place in it and the surrounding parts of the flower, the result being the production of the fruit. The fruit essentially consists of the mature ovary or ovaries containing the impregnated ovule or ovules, which are then termed seeds. All fruits are composed of two parts, namely, of a shell called the *pericarp* (fig. 2, *p*), and *seed* or *seeds* contained within it.

The *seed* or impregnated ovule, is essentially com-posed of two parts, namely, of a *nucleus* or *kernel* (figs. 1 and 2), and *integuments* or *seed-coats* (fig. 2, *t*). There are commonly two seed-coats, and the nucleus may either consist entirely of an embryo or rudimentary plant (fig. 1), which is alone essential to it ; or of the embryo surrounded by nourishing matter called the *albumen* (fig. 2, *a*). The parts of the embryo having already been described, as well as the mode in which the fundamental organs of the future plant are developed from them, as also the general characters of these organs, we need not further allude to them at present, except to remark that the organs as thus defined are only found in the most highly developed plants, and that such plants are called Phanerogamous or Phæno-gamous, literally plants with evident sexual organs.

Such plants are also called Flowering, and, as already noticed, are divided into two classes called Dicotyledons and Monocotyledons. The third class of plants, also previously noticed as comprising Ferns, Mosses, Sea-weeds, &c., having no true flowers or seeds, and therefore without cotyledons, are termed Acotyledons. They are also called Flowerless and Cryptogamous plants, because they have no true flowers furnished with stamens and carpels. By the differences thus presented by plants we divide the Vegetable Kingdom at first into two subkingdoms, as follows :—1. Phanerogamia, Cotyledones, or Flowering. 2. Cryptogamia, Acotyledones, or Flowerless. The former being again divided into two classes, the Monocotyledones and the Dicotyledones, and the latter constituting a class by themselves called the Acotyledones. Our future remarks will more especially apply to the Flowering Plants, the organs of which, after this introductory sketch, we now proceed to describe more in detail and in their proper order.

QUESTIONS.

INTRODUCTORY.

1. What is the object of Natural History?
2. What are the three kingdoms of nature?
3. What do you mean by Organic and Inorganic?
4. What is Botany, and what does its study embrace?
5. What is meant by Organography?
6. Explain the meaning of Morphology.
7. What is Structural Botany?
8. Of what does the seed of the Almond consist?
9. What is the embryo?
10. Describe the parts of the embryo.
11. Are there always two cotyledons in the embryo?
12. Define the meaning of the terms Dicotyledons, Monocotyledons, and Acotyledons, as applied to the three great classes of plants.
13. Describe the growth of the embryo; and say what the process is called.
14. What are the fundamental organs of a plant, and why are they so called?
15. What is meant by an organ of nutrition?
16. What is meant by an organ of reproduction?

I.—ORGANS OF NUTRITION.

17. Define the root.
18. Define the stem.

19. What is a leaf-bud?
20. What are the essential characters which distinguish a stem from a root?
21. What are branches and twigs?
22. Define the leaf.
23. What is a node?
24. Mention and describe the parts of the leaf.
25. Which is the part of the leaf most commonly present?

II.—ORGANS OF REPRODUCTION.

26. What is a peduncle, and what are pedicels?
27. What are bracts?
28. What is meant by the inflorescence?
29. Of what does a flower consist?
30. What is the thalamus?
31. In what order are the parts of the flower arranged upon the thalamus?
32. Define the calyx.
33. What are the parts of the calyx?
34. Define the corolla.
35. What are the parts of the corolla, and how are they known?
36. What is the perianth? Give an example?
37. Why are the floral envelopes called non-essential organs?
38. What do you understand by apetalous and naked flowers?
39. What is meant by the Androecium? Mention and describe its parts.
40. What is meant by the Gynoecium? Mention and describe its parts.
41. What is the pistil?
42. Why are the stamens and carpels called essential organs?
43. What are unisexual flowers, and how are they defined?
44. How is the fruit formed, and of what does it essentially consist?
45. What are the parts of the fruit?
46. What is the seed, and of what does it consist?
47. What are the constituent parts of the nucleus?
48. What is meant by Phanerogamous plants?
49. What is meant by Cryptogamous plants?
50. What are the two sub-kingdoms of plants?
51. What are the classes of plants?

CHAPTER II.

ORGANS OF NUTRITION.

SECTION I.—THE ROOT OR DESCENDING AXIS.

The root, as previously defined, is that part of the plant which at its first development in the embryo

B 2

takes a downward direction, in consequence of which it is called the descending axis, avoiding the light and air, and fixing the plant to the earth, or to the substance upon which it grows; or floating in the water, when the plant grows on the surface of that medium. Its office is especially to obtain food in a liquid state, which is carried up by it and the stem to the leaves, by which the plant is subsequently nourished. The point of junction of the root and stem is called the Neck. The extremities of the main root and its branches are commonly termed *spongioles* or *spongelets*.

Roots are distinguished from stems by several characters (only two of which can be now noticed), as follows :—

1. Roots are known from stems by their direction, as they grow downwards, while stems have an upward direction (fig. 8, *r*).

2. A stem has on its surface a number of leaves, symmetrically arranged, and in the angle called the axil, formed by the juxtaposition of each leaf with the stem there is placed a bud (fig. 4, *b*), which is capable, as will be hereafter particularly noticed, of growing into a branch, which will be covered in like manner with other leaves and buds, themselves again capable of shooting into branches. Consequently, as the branches of a stem can only proceed from the axils of leaves thus symmetrically arranged, they must of necessity be also symmetrical in their arrangement. Roots, on the contrary, have neither leaves nor buds, and have therefore no provision for a regular branching, but they divide and sub-divide as occasion requires, and without any disposition to assume a symmetrical character.

The roots of most plants grow in the earth or in water ; but some plants develop roots from their stems in the air, hence such are termed aerial roots. The simplest roots of this kind are seen in the Ivy (fig. 13, *a a*), and some other climbing plants, where they are especially intended for their mechanical support, In the

Banyan or Indian Fig-tree these aerial roots are developed to a remarkable extent from the branches, and
by ultimately reaching
the soil, they form so
many natural supports
by which this plant is
enabled to spread over
a large area.

In some plants, as
certain Orchids, none
but aerial roots are pro-
duced; and as these never
reach the soil, they can-
not obtain any nourish-
ment from it, but must
draw it entirely from the
air in which they are
placed, and hence they
are termed *Air Plants;*
or as they commonly
grow upon other plants,
although they obtain no
nourishment from them,
they are also called *Epiphytes.*

There are some plants
which not only grow upon
others, but which send
their roots into the sub-
stance of those on which
they are placed, and de-
rive their nourishment
from them, just as the
roots of ordinary plants
obtain food from the
earth, and those of air-
plants from the air.
Such plants are called
Parasites, of which the Mistletoe forms a good example.

Fig. 13

Fig.13.—Common Ivy: *aa,* aerial roots.

Such plants, by living partially or entirely upon those on which they are placed, frequently destroy them, and thus do immense damage to Clover, Flax, and other crops in this country and elsewhere. In some countries the flowers of these parasites grow to an enormous size, as is the case with the Rafflesia, a native of Sumatra. Thus, the first flower which was discovered of this plant measured nine feet in circumference, and weighed fifteen pounds. This is by far the largest flower of any known plant; that of the beautiful Victoria Water Lily, now well-known under cultivation amongst the stove plants in this country, sinks into insignificance when compared with it, no flower of it having been produced exceeding twelve inches in diameter, or about three feet in circumference.

VARIETIES AND FORMS OF ROOTS.—There are two varieties

Fig. 14.　　　　　Fig. 15.　　　　　Fig. 16.

Fig. 14.—Carrot Root.
Fig. 15.—Radish Root.
Fig. 16.—Turnip Root.

of roots, namely, the *True* or *Primary*, and the *Adventitious* or *Secondary*. The *primary root* is only produced by the direct elongation of the radicle of the embryo, and as such is generally found with a central axis or trunk, from which the branches are given off in an irregular manner (fig. 3). This is commonly called a *tap-root*, and has various forms, as *conical* (fig. 14), *fusiform* (fig. 15), *napiform* (fig. 16). The *adventitious root*, instead of proceeding from a definite point, is, to a certain extent at least, accidental in its origin, and dependent upon favourable external circumstances for its development. All roots of monocotyledonous and acotyledonous plants, as well as aerial roots, and roots of all modifications of stems, slips, and cuttings of plants, &c., are of this nature. Such roots are generally of small size, and given off in variable numbers (fig. 25), and are commonly described as *fibrous*.

Fig. 17.

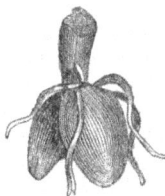

Fig. 17.—Tubercular root of an Orchis.

Sometimes the divisions of roots become enlarged, and act as reservoirs of nutriment, as in the common Orchis (fig. 17). These enlarged portions are called *tubercules*, and the root is said to be *tubercular*.

QUESTIONS.

1. Define the root, and mention its office.
2. What is the Neck, and what are spongioles?
3. What are the distinctive characters of roots and stems?
4. What is the meaning of axil?
5. What is meant by aerial roots? Give examples.
6. What are epiphytes or air-plants? Give an example.
7. What are parasites? Give an example.
8. How do parasites injure the plants upon which they grow?
9. What plant produces the largest flower known?
10. What is the difference between a true or primary, and an adventitious or secondary root?
11. What is a tap-root, and what are its common forms?
12. Give examples of adventitious roots.
13. What are fibrous roots?
14. What are tubercules?

SECTION II.—THE STEM OR ASCENDING AXIS.

The stem is defined as that part of the axis of a plant which grows in an opposite direction to the root, for while the root grows downwards the stem developes in an upward direction (from which cause it is called the ascending axis), seeking the light and air, and bearing on its surface the leaves and other leafy appendages (fig. 8, *s*).

The stem has received many names, according to its nature. Thus it is called a *caulis* in plants which are *herbaceous*, or die down annually; a *trunk*, as in trees, where it is woody and perennial; a *culm*, as in most grasses and sedges, where it presents a jointed appearance; and a *caudex* or *stipe*, as in tree-ferns and palms.

In form the stem is generally more or less cylindrical, but in many cases it becomes angular, and in some plants, particularly in certain Cacti and Orchids, it assumes a variety of other shapes, as rounded or oval, globular, more or less flattened, columnar, &c.

In general, stems possess a firm texture, and can readily sustain themselves in an upright direction; but in other instances they are too weak to support themselves, and thus require the aid of some other body. In such cases, if they trail on the ground, they are said to be *prostrate* or *procumbent* (fig. 28); or if they take an erect position, and cling to neighbouring objects for support, they are called *climbing* if they proceed in a more or less straight direction, as in the Passion-flower (fig. 18), where they cling to other bodies by means of little twisted ramifications called tendrils, *v v;* or in the Ivy, where they emit little root-like processes from their sides, by which they adhere to neighbouring objects (fig. 18, *a a*). But if such stems twist round other bodies in a spiral manner, they are said to be *twining*, as in some Convolvuli, the French Bean, Honeysuckle (fig. 19), and Hop.

From the nature, duration, and mode of branching of their stems, plants have been divided from the earliest period into three classes, called respectively *Herbs*, *Shrubs*, and *Trees*. Thus, those plants which have

Fig. 19.

Fig. 18.

Fig. 18.—Stem of a species of Passion-flower: *v v*, tendrils. Fig. 19.—Twining stem of Honeysuckle, with buds on its surface.

stems that die down annually to the surface of the ground are called *herbs;* while those with perennial aerial woody stems are termed *trees* or *shrubs* according to circumstances. Thus the term tree is applied if the branches are perennial, and arise from a trunk; but when the branches are perennial, and proceed directly from or near to the surface of the ground, without any supporting trunk, or where this is very short, a *shrub* is formed, and this, when low and very much branched at the base, is called a *bush*.

BUDS.—We have already stated that the presence of leaves and leaf-buds essentially distinguishes a stem from a root. The leaves will be treated of hereafter; but we must now describe the nature of buds, and the mode in which branches are formed. We have also seen that leaves are always developed at regular points on the surface of the stem called *nodes*, the intervals between the nodes being termed *internodes*, and that under ordinary circumstances one or more buds are developed in the axil of every leaf (figs. 4, *b*, and 20). In like manner, the apex of a stem, as well as of all its divisions

Fig. 20.

Fig. 20.—Buds of the Horse-chestnut, one of which has a scar below which has been produced by the falling of a leaf.

which are capable of further growth in a longitudinal direction, are also terminated by a similar bud (fig. 24, 1). The former are called *lateral* or *axillary*, and the latter *terminal*, buds. Each bud, whether lateral or terminal, consists, 1st, of a central growing point, which is composed of similar tissues to the stem or branch on which it is placed, in fact, is a direct prolongation of these tissues; and 2nd, of rudimentary leaves surrounding this growing point, and arranged symmetrically over one another. Such is the ordinary structure of buds as found in this country in seedlings or plants which only live during the warmer seasons of the year, as also of those commonly of plants which inhabit warmer regions; but in perennial plants of temperate and cold climates, where the buds are dormant during the winter, and consequently exposed to all its rigours, we generally find certain protective organs on their outer surface in the form of modified leaves, or parts of leaves, which are commonly called *scales*. These scales are usually of a hardened texture, and are sometimes covered with a resinous secretion, as in the Horse-chestnut and several kinds of Poplars, or with a dense coating of soft hairs, as in many Willows. Such protective organs, therefore, prevent the inner delicate rudimentary leaves and grow-ing point from being injured by cold, and by the other injurious influences to which they are necessarily sub-jected. These latter buds are commonly termed *scaly,* while those without protective organs are called *naked.*

The bud thus contains all the elements of a stem or branch; in reality it is the first stage of their growth, the axis being here so short that the rudimentary leaves are close together, and therefore overlap one another. When further growth takes place, as in the spring, the internodes, or spaces between the leaves, become de-veloped, and thus the leaves become separated from each other, much in the same way as the joints of a telescope (which may be regarded as representing the nodes), become separated from each other by lengths of tube, representing the internodes, when it is drawn out. Under ordinary circumstances, by the develop-ment of terminal buds, the main stem and its branches increase in length, and by the growth of lateral buds branches are produced. But buds are also capable of being removed from one plant and made to grow upon another of a nearly allied nature. Thus the operations of Budding and Grafting depend for their success upon this circumstance. In some instances, also, a bud may be even made to grow in the soil, and produce a new plant, as in the process of *layering.* In this latter process, the gardener bends down a portion of a plant, upon which one bud at least is placed, into the earth; this bud is at first supported by nourishment derived from its parent, but it soon produces roots, and thus acquires the power of obtaining food for itself, and may be accordingly then separated from its parent, and form a distinct plant.

In the same manner as branches are produced from lateral buds placed on the main axis or stem, so also from the axillary buds situated on these branches other buds and branches are formed; these, again, will form other buds and branches, and so on, every successive branch forming other branches in like manner. The main divisions of the stem are commonly known as *branches*, while the smaller subdivisions of the branches are termed *twigs*. As the branches are thus produced from the axils of leaves, and as these are always arranged in a more or less symmetrical manner on a stem or branch, it follows that the branches of a stem are also symmetrically placed. This constitutes, as already noticed (see Root), one of the characters which distinguishes a stem from a root, as the latter organ has no provision for symmetrical branching.

This corresponding symmetry between the arrangement of the branches and leaves is, however, frequently interfered with from various causes: as the non-development of axillary buds; their arrest in development, by which *knots* are formed in the wood instead of branches; the development of other buds from various points besides the axils of leaves, and in other ways. At other times a bud, instead of developing as usual, so as to form a leaf-bearing branch, becomes arrested in its growth, and forms a hardened projection, terminating in a more or less acute point, as in the Hawthorn. Such an irregularly developed branch is called a *spine* or *thorn*. That spines are modified branches is proved by their structure being exactly the same as the stem or branch upon which they are placed, by their sometimes bearing leaves, as in the Sloe, and by their being frequently changed into ordinary leaf-bearing branches by cultivation, as in the Apple and Pear,

Fig 21.

Fig. 21.—Prickles *p p*, on a branch of the Rose.

and in other ways. Spines are also frequently confounded with certain hardened sharp-pointed processes
springing from the external parts of a plant, as in
Brambles and Roses (fig. 21, *p p*), and which are termed
prickles. These are, however, at once distinguished
from spines by being merely superficial appendages—
that is, having no connection with the internal parts of
the stem or branch.

Another irregular formed branch is the *tendril*, as
seen in the Vine and Passion-flower (fig. 18, *v v*). This
is defined as a thread-like leafless branch, which is
twisted in a spiral direction; it is one of those con-
trivances of nature by means of which weak plants are
enabled to rise into the air by attaching themselves to
neighbouring bodies for support.

KINDS OF STEM AND BRANCHES.—We have already
seen that the stem, when first developed from the
embryo, always takes a direction upwards into the air—
that is, directly opposite to that of the root. This
direction is more commonly continued throughout the
life of the plant; but in many plants this original direction of the stem is deviated from at an early period,
and it passes along, or partly under, the surface of the
ground, and even in many cases, contrary to what commonly occurs, stems withdraw entirely from the light
and air, and even live under ground like roots, with
which they are consequently commonly confounded. All
such stems are, however, readily distinguished from
roots either by the presence of leaves and buds, or by
scales or modified leaves, or by the presence of scars
on their surface produced by the falling off of former
leaves or buds (fig. 22, *s*). In this manner many
irregular kinds of stem are produced, of which some
of the more important will be now noticed.

Of these one of the commonest is the *Rhizome* or
Rootstock (fig. 22). This is a prostrate thickened
stem or branch which creeps along the surface of the
ground, or more generally partly beneath it, and gives
off buds from its upper surface and roots from its lower.

Such a stem is found in the Fern, Iris, Ginger Plant, Turmeric, Sweet Flag, and many other plants. Such stems often creep for a long distance, and have their upper surface marked by scars produced by the falling off of former leaves or branches, by which character they may be commonly distinguished, even when in a dried state, from roots.

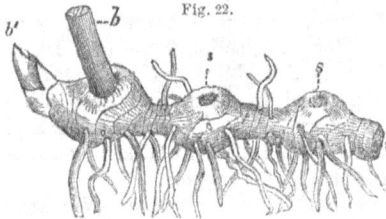

Fig. 22.—Portion of rhizome, r, of the Solomon's Seal; b′, terminal bud; b, a branch; s s, scars produced by the decay of old branches.

Another kind of irregular stem is seen in the Strawberry Plant, where the main stem sends off from its base a slender lengthened prostrate branch (fig. 23), which gives off at its end leaves and roots, and thus produces a new plant, which in like manner extends itself. This kind of stem is called a *runner*.

Fig. 23.—A portion of the Strawberry plant: a, an axis producing a tuft of leaves, r, at its end, from the axil of one of which another axis or runner, a″, arises, bearing a rudimentary leaf, f, near the middle, and a cluster of leaves, r, at its end; a‴, a third axis, produced in a similar manner to the former; f f, roots.

These two kinds of stem are either entirely aerial, or partly developed in the air and partly under ground; the remaining kinds of stem to be noticed are essentially subterranean like roots.

The Creeping Stem. This is a slender branch which creeps along beneath the surface of the earth, emitting roots from its lower side and buds from its upper, like the rhizome, from which, however, it is distinguished by its slender form and entirely subterranean course. The Sand Sedge (fig. 24) and Couch Grass afford good examples of this stem. In some instances such stems serve important purposes in nature; thus those of the Sand Sedge, by spreading through the sand of the sea-shore, and in this way binding it together, prevent it from

Fig. 24.

Fig. 24.—Creeping stem of the Sand Sedge: 1, terminal bud by which the stem continues to lengthen; 2, 3, 4, shoots produced from former buds.

being washed away by the receding waves. Others, like the Couch Grass, are the pest of the agriculturist, who finds it very difficult to destroy them by cutting into pieces, for as every node is capable of developing a leaf-bud and roots, each of the pieces into which it is thus divided is capable of becoming an independent individual, and therefore such a process, instead of destroying the plant, only serves the purpose of still further multiplying it, by placing the separated portions under more favourable conditions for development.

One of the most irregular forms of such stems is seen in the Potato and Jerusalem Artichoke. This kind of stem is called a *tuber*. This is a subterranean branch arrested in its growth and very much enlarged by the deposition of starch and other nutritious substances in its interior. That the tuber is in reality a stem is proved by its having on its surface, or more or less buried in its substance, a number of irregularly developed buds, or eyes as they are commonly called, from which new plants are ultimately formed. This stem-like nature of the tuber is also clearly proved by the practice commonly adopted for propagating potatoes, the tuber being cut into pieces, each of which contains one or more eyes. These eyes, when placed under favourable circumstances for development, are at first nourished by the matter which surrounds them, by which they are enabled to put forth roots, and obtain nourishment for themselves, and thus form independent plants.

Fig. 25.

Fig. 25.—Scaly bulb of the Lily: *a*, shortened stem ; *b*, fibrous roots ; *c*, scales ; *d*, flowering stem.

The *bulb*, as seen in the Lily, Onion, Tulip, Hyacinth, and many other plants, is another kind of subterranean stem. It is defined as a shortened stem or branch, which is generally reduced to a rounded or somewhat flattened plate (fig. 25, *a*), which bears on its surface a number of fleshy scales, *c*, or modified leaves, which, like the ordinary leaves of a branch, frequently develop in their axils new bulbs called by gardeners cloves, and their presence is a proof at once of the stem-like nature of a bulb. Or we may consider a bulb as a subterranean bud of a scaly nature, which sends off roots from below (fig. 25, *b*), and a stem upwards bearing leaves and flowers, *d*.

In the Onion and Hyacinth (fig. 26), the inner scales, which are thick and fleshy, enclose each other in a concentric manner, are covered externally by thin membranous ones, which form a covering or *tunic* to them, and hence bulbs of such a nature are termed *tunicated* or *coated*. Other bulbs, such as the Lily (fig. 25), have all the scales thick and fleshy, and so arranged as to overlap each other only, like the leaves of an ordinary bud; such are called *naked* or *scaly* bulbs.

The subterranean stems of the Crocus, Colchicum, and other plants, have a consider-

Fig. 26.

Fig. 26.—The Wild Hyacinth, showing bulb, *b*, inflorescence, *inf*, and leaves, *l*.

able resemblance to bulbs, with which, in common language, they are ordinarily confounded; but they are readily distinguished by their more solid nature. Such stems are called *corms*. A *corm* is defined as a solid subterranean stem of a rounded or somewhat oval figure, and commonly covered externally by thin membranous scales, and giving off one or more buds or young corms from the apex, as in the Crocus, or from the side, as in the Colchicum. Practically, a corm may be distinguished from a bulb by its solid nature, the bulb being formed of imbricated scales.

Both bulbs and corms are only found in monocoty-ledonous plants.

QUESTIONS.

1. Define the stem.
2. Describe the following stems:—caulis, trunk, culm, and caudex or stipe.
8. Mention the various forms of stems.
4. What are prostrate or procumbent, climbing, and twining stems?
5. What are herbs, shrubs, and trees?
6. What is meant by a bush?
7. What are nodes and internodes?
8. Where are buds placed, and what terms are applied to them from their different positions?
9. Describe a bud.
10. What is the difference between the bud of an herbaceous plant or that of a plant of warm regions, and of a bud exposed to the cold of winter?
11. Describe the nature of *scales*, and explain what is meant by scaly and naked buds.
12. Explain the growth of a bud into a branch.
13. How do stems and branches increase in length?
14. Explain the operations of budding, grafting, and layering.
15. Explain the process of branching, and show why branches are symmetrically arranged.
16. What causes interfere with the symmetrical arrangement of branches?
17. What are twigs and knots?
18. What is a spine or thorn, and how is it produced?
19. How are spines distinguished from prickles?
20. What is a tendril, and what is its use?

KINDS OF STEM AND BRANCHES.

21. How are stems which run along, or burrow under the ground, to be distinguished from roots?
22. Define a rhizome or rootstock, and give examples.

23. How are rhizomes when in a dried state to be distinguished from roots?

24. Define a runner. Give an example.

25. Define a creeping stem.

26. Give examples of creeping stems, and show what purposes they serve in nature, and with what difficulty they are destroyed.

27. Define a tuber, and give examples.

28. How is the tuber proved to be a kind of stem?

29. Define a bulb, and give examples. What are cloves?

30. Describe tunicated and scaly bulbs.

31. What is a corm?

32. How is a corm distinguished from a bulb?

33. In what class of plants are bulbs and corms alone found?

SECTION III.—THE LEAF.

Having now finished the description of the axis or central portion of the plant, we are able to describe the leaves and other organs which succeed them, all of which are placed on the stem or ascending axis. These are termed, collectively, appendages of the axis; and, individually, leaves, flowers and their parts, and fruit. Of all these, the leaves alone are organs of nutrition, the remaining organs being directly or indirectly connected with the process of reproduction. We must first describe the leaf.

The *leaf* is defined as being usually a green more or less flattened expansion of the stem or one of its branches; but exceptions to both these characters occur in different plants. Thus in Stone-crop, Aloes, and many other plants, the leaves are thick and fleshy, when they are termed *succulent;* while in other plants, as Broomrapes, they present a brown scaly appearance; and in underground buds or bulbs they are colourless and fleshy (fig. 25, *c*).

The part of the stem or branch from which a leaf arises is called a *node*, and the space between two nodes an *internode.* The portion of the leaf nearest to the axis from which it arises is called the *base*, the opposite extremity the *apex*, and the lines connecting the base and apex the *margins.* The angle formed by the union of the upper surface of the leaf with the stem, as already noticed, is called the *axil;* and everything arising out of that point, as for instance a bud (fig. 4, *b*), is said to be axillary to the leaf.

Leaves commonly fall off after they have performed their functions, but their duration varies in different plants, and they receive different names accordingly. More commonly the leaf lasts throughout the season in which it is developed, when it is *deciduous;* or if beyond a single season, or until new leaves are formed, so that the plant is never without leaves, as in the common cherry laurel of our shrubberies and gardens, it is *persistent*, and the plant is called *evergreen.*

When a leaf separates from the stem, without leaving any trace of its existence, except a scar (fig. 20) at the point of disruption, as in the Chestnut, it is said to be *articulated;* or if it decays gradually upon it, so that portions remain upon the stem for some time, as in Grasses and Ferns, it is *non-articulated.*

The leaf, in its highest state of development, as already noticed (see page 12), consists of three distinct parts, called respectively *lamina* or *blade, petiole* or *leaf-stalk,* and *stipular portion.* These three parts are by no means always present, although such is frequently the case, as in the Water Pepper (fig. 5) and Trailing Willow (fig. 6); but in numerous plants one of these parts is absent, and in some two, the leaf being in such instances reduced to two or one of its portions only. The petiole and the stipular portion are those which are more commonly absent; in the former case, the leaf is termed *sessile* (fig. 32); in the latter, it is *exstipulate* (fig. 33). The blade of the leaf is that portion which is not only the one most commonly present, but it is that which is generally most developed, and performs the more important functions of the leaf; and in ordinary language it is spoken of under the name of leaf. Sometimes the blade is divided into two or more separate parts, when it is called *compound* (fig. 54); or if there is but one blade (fig. 27), it is said to be *simple.*

1. INSERTION AND ARRANGEMENT OF LEAVES.

Leaves are variously inserted and arranged upon the stem or branch, and receive different names accordingly.

a. Insertion.—When a leaf arises from the stem by

Fig. 27.   Fig. 29.

Fig. 28.

Fig. 27.—Peltate leaf of the Indian Cress. Fig 28.—Amplexicaul petiole. Fig. 29.—Scotch Thistle, with decurrent leaves, *l*; *f*, flowers forming a head or capitulum, and surrounded by an involucre, *b*.

means of a stalk, it is said to be *stalked* or *petiolate* (fig. 6, *p*), as in the Lilac; or when the stalk is attached to the blade within the margin, as in the Indian Cress (fig. 27), it is termed *peltate* or *shield-shaped*; when the blade arises directly from the stem without a stalk (fig. 32), it is *sessile*; when a leaf is enlarged at its base, so as to clasp the stem more or less, it is *embracing* or *amplexicaul* (fig. 28), as in the Parsley ; or if it forms a complete sheath around the stem as in Grasses (fig. 58, *g*), it is *sheathing*.   When a leaf is prolonged

Fig. 30.   Fig. 31.

Fig. 30.—Common Hare's-ear, with perfoliate leaves : *u*, umbel.
Fig. 31.—Common Yellow-wort, with connate leaves ; the flowers are arranged in a cymose manner.

from its base so as to form a leafy appendage down the stem, as in Thistles (fig. 29), it is *decurrent;* when the two margins or sides of a leaf project beyond the stem and unite, as in the Hare's-ear (fig. 30), it is *perfoliate;* and when two leaves placed on opposite sides of the stem unite by their base, as in some Honeysuckles, they are termed *connate* (fig. 31).

b. Arrangement.—When only one leaf arises from a node on a lengthened axis, the leaves are said to be *alternate,* as in the Ivy (fig. 13), because they succeed each other alternately on different sides of the axis; but when two leaves arise from a node they are called *opposite* (fig. 33), because they are then situated on opposite sides of the axis; or when three or more leaves arise from the stem so as to be arranged around it in the form of a circle, they are called *whorled* or *verticillate* (fig. 32), and each circle is termed a *whorl* or *verticil.* When leaves are opposite, the successive

Fig. 32.   Fig. 33.

Fig. 32.—Common Mare's-tail with whorled sessile leaves. Fig. 33 —Decussate leaves.

pairs as they succeed each other commonly cross at right angles, when they are said to *decussate* (fig. 33) as in the Lilac. When the internodes of the main axis or stem are very short, the leaves are called *radical*, as in the Primrose, because they arise at, or below the surface of the ground, and thus apparently form the root; and when the internodes of an axillary branch are non-developed all the leaves of that branch are brought into contact, and they then form a *tuft* or *fascicle*, as in the Larch (fig. 101).

The general term *vernation* (spring state) is applied to the arrangement of the leaves in an unexpanded or rudimentary condition in the bud. Of this there are several modifications, but these are too complicated to be described to the young student.

2. SURFACE OF LEAVES.

The surfaces of leaves as well as the stem, and all its appendages, are either quite smooth, or *glabrous* as it is termed, or provided with various appendages which have no connection with the internal tissues of the plant. These appendages are of various kinds, but they may be all arranged under the two heads of *Hairs* or non-secreting organs, and *Glands* or secreting organs.

a. Hairs.—These are thread-like prolongations from the surface of plants of various forms, as *conical, cylindrical, necklace-shaped, hooked,* &c.; and either undivided, forked, or branched. In other cases they become modified, and form little membranous bodies looking like chaff or bran, when they are called *scales* or *scurf;* or they form stiffened processes or *bristles;* or large hardened appendages terminating in a sharp point, when they are termed *prickles* (fig. 21), as in the Rose.

The varying abundance and character of hairs and their modifications give different appearances to the surface of the leaves, all of which are distinguished by special names, and are important in practical botany, as *pilose* or slightly hairy, *hispid*, with hard rough bristles, *woolly, cottony, silky,* &c., all of which terms sufficiently explain themselves, being used in their ordinary acceptation.

· *b. Glands.*—The term gland is applied to the hair-like bodies placed on the surface of leaves and other organs, which contain secretions, as oils or resinous matters; or to cavities placed below the surface containing similar secretions, and which may be readily observed in many leaves, such as those of the Orange and Myrtle, by holding them up to the light, when they appear as little transparent dots. Such leaves are termed *dotted*.

Stings are also a kind of gland, and consist of a hair enlarged at its base (fig. 34, *b*), and filled by an irritating fluid, and terminating above in a somewhat rounded head, *s*. When the knob-like head is broken off by a gentle touch, the sharp point of the sting which then remains, enters the skin, and the irritating fluid is pushed up at the same time into the wound; but when a nettle sting is grasped firmly, instead of being touched lightly, the sting becomes crushed, and, as it cannot then enter the skin, no irritation is produced.

Fig. 34.

Fig. 34.—Sting of the Common Nettle.

3. PARTS OF LEAVES.

We have already stated that the most highly developed leaves consisted of three parts: namely, of a *lamina* or *blade*, a *petiole* or *stalk*, and a *stipular* portion (see page 12, and figs. 5 and 6). We have now to describe each of these parts more in detail.

A. LAMINA OR BLADE.

VENATION.—If you hold up the blade of a leaf between your eye and the light, it is seen, in most cases, to be traversed by lines which vary in number and

direction in different leaves.   These lines are caused
by the framework or skeleton of the leaf—namely, that
portion which is left when leaves are macerated in
water for a length of time, whilst the soft pulp, which
in the living leaf contains green matter, is destroyed.
The distribution of these lines, which are called *veins*,
is termed *venation*.

The arrangement of these veins varies much in the
leaves of different plants, and corresponding names are
given accordingly.   Thus, when there is one large central vein proceeding from the base to the apex of the
lamina from which all the other veins proceed, this is
called the *mid-
rib* (fig. 36);
or when there
are three or
more large
veins thus pro-
ceeding from
the base to the
apex, or to the
margins (fig.
35) of the
blade, the sepa-
rate veins are
then termed
ribs. The divi-
sions or pri-
mary branches
of the midrib,
or of the sepa-
rate ribs, are
c o m m o n l y
called *veins*,
and their smal-
ler branches
veinlets.

Fig. 35.

Fig. 35.—Leaf of Occidental Plane.

When the
blade has a midrib giving off veins on each side,

arranged like the barbs of a feather, such a blade (or leaf, as it is commonly called) is said to be *feather-veined* or *pinnately-veined* (figs. 36 and 43); but when there are three or more ribs which diverge from each other as they pass through the blade, like the fingers when they are spread out from the palm of the hand, the leaf is termed *palmate - veined* or *radiate-veined* (figs. 35 and 46). In both these kinds of venation, and in all cases where the main veins are connected by a network of veins, the venation is said to be *netted* or *reticulated*, and is characteristic of dicotyledonous plants; but if there is no such network (fig. 37), the leaf is said to be *parallel-veined*, as is commonly the case in the leaves of monocotyledons. When acotyledonous plants have leaves, as is the case in Ferns, the veins commonly divide in a forked manner (fig 38), and the venation is therefore called *forked*.

Fig. 36.

Fig. 36.—Leaf of the Common Elm.

Fig. 37.

Fig. 38.

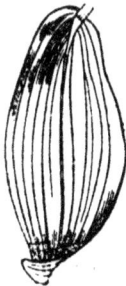

Fig. 37.—Orchis Leaf with paralle venation. Fig. 38.— Forked venation of a Fern leaf.

COMPOSITION.—As already noticed, leaves are divided into *simple* and *compound*, the former term being applied when there is only one blade (figs. 35—37), however much this may be divided, so long as the divisions are attached by a broad base to the midrib (figs. 41 and 42) or petiole (fig. 46) from which they spring; but when the leaf is composed of two or more entirely distinct portions, each bearing the same relation to the petiole as the petiole itself does to the stem from whence it arises (fig. 54), it is termed *compound*. The separated portions of a compound leaf are then called *leaflets*, and these may be either sessile or stalked. In the latter case the main axis which supports the leaflets is called the *common petiole*, and the stalk of each leaflet a *partial petiole*.

1. SIMPLE LEAVES.—Such leaves present numerous modifications as regards the shape, form, margin, apex, &c., of their blades, hence we have a number of terms in use to define them. The leaflets of compound leaves, the stipules, and all flattened organs of the plant, such as bracts, sepals, petals, &c., are subject to like variations; and as the same terms are in all cases employed, it is necessary that we should at once describe the more important of them.

a. Margin.—If the edge or margin of a blade is perfectly even, it is said to be *entire* (fig. 37); but when the margin has sharp projections or teeth, and all point towards the apex of the blade, it is *serrate* (fig. 39); or if the teeth are sharp, but do not point in any definite direction, the margin is *dentate* or *toothed* (fig. 35); when the teeth are rounded the margin is *crenate* (fig. 38); when the edge of a blade curves slightly outward and inward (fig. 40) it is said to be *wavy;* or when the margin is twisted and curled it is *crisped.*

These different kinds of margin are also themselves liable to modifications, some of which are important. Thus, if the teeth of a serrate margin are themselves serrate we use the term *biserrate* (fig. 36), or when the margin is minutely serrate it is called *serrulate;*

when the teeth of a crenate margin are very small the blade is *crenulate*, or if the teeth be themselves crenate it is *bicrenate*; and when the teeth of a dentate margin are themselves toothed the margin is *doubly-toothed*.

Fig. 39.

Fig. 40.

Fig. 39.—Leaf of Black Poplar. Fig. 40.—Spiny leaf of the common Holly.

b. Incision.—This term is applied when the margin of a blade is more deeply divided than in the instances just given under the head of margin. The divisions are then commonly called *lobes*, and the spaces between them *fissures*, or in composition the term *-fid* is used, and the leaf is said to be *cleft* (fig. 43). In describing such leaves we either say they are *bifid* or *two-cleft*, *trifid* or *three-cleft*, *quinquefid* or *five-cleft*, *multifid* or *many-cleft*, &c., according to the number of their fissures; or *two-lobed*, *three-lobed*, *five-lobed*, *many-lobed*, &c., &c., from the number of lobes.

Sometimes, when the blade is more deeply divided—that is, nearly to the base or midrib (fig. 42), we call the divisions *partitions*, and the leaf is said to be *partite;* or if divided quite to the midrib or base (fig. 41), the term *segments* is used, and the leaf is *-sected*.

As the divisions of the blade are always arranged

Fig. 41.   Fig. 42.   Fig. 43.

Figs. 41 and 42.—Leaves or fronds of Mountain Fern.
Fig. 43.—Leaf of Oak.

in the direction of the principal veins, the leaf is more accurately defined by using terms derived from the mode of venation combined with that of division, than by terms indicating simply the number of fissures, lobes, &c. Thus, if the blade is pinnately-veined the divisions are correspondingly placed, and the leaf is *pinnatifid* (fig. 43), *pinnatipartite* (fig. 42), or *pinnatisected* (fig. 41), according to their depth ; or when palmately-veined and divided accordingly the leaf is *palmatifid*, *palmatipartite*, or *palmatisected*, in like manner. When the divisions are themselves divided in a similar manner to the blade itself the leaf is *bipinnatifid*, &c., the application of which terms will be readily understood without further explanation.

Certain modifications of both pinnately-veined and palmately-veined leaves have also received special names, the more important of which are the *lyrate*, *runcinate*, *palmate*, *digitate*, and *pedate*. Thus a leaf is *lyrate* (fig. 45) when the terminal lobe is large and rounded, and the lateral lobes gradually smaller towards the base; it is

runcinate (fig. 44) when the terminal lobe is large and triangular,and the lateral lobes point backward toward the base; it is properly termed *palmate* (fig. 85) when there are five spreading lobes, and thus resembling the hand with its spreading fingers; and *digitate* under the same circum-

Fig. 44.

Fig. 44.—Dandelion Plant: *l*, leaves; *f*, flowers; *i*, involucre ; *p*, fruits, crowned with feathery pappus ; *r*, receptacle.

stances when the lobes are narrow. Some botanists, however, use these terms indifferently. When the lateral lobes at the base of a divided palmately-veined leaf are themselves lobed (fig. 46), so that the whole somewhat resembles a bird's foot, the leaf is *pedate* or *pedatifid*.

Fig. 45.   Fig. 46.

Fig. 45.—Lyrate leaf of the common Turnip. Fig. 46.—Pedate leaf of Hellebore.

c. Apex.—When the blade is rounded at the apex it is *obtuse* (fig. 50); when it terminates in a broad,

Fig. 47.   Fig. 48.

shallow notch it is *retuse*; when with a sharp, somewhat triangular notch (fig. 47) *emarginate;* when cut off at the apex it is *truncate;* when it is more or less rounded and tipped abruptly with a short stiff sharp point (fig. 48) it is *mucronate;* when the apex gradually ends in a point it is *acute* (fig. 86); or when the point is long

Fig. 47.—Oval leaf, emarginate at the apex. Fig. 48.—Obovate leaf, with a mucronate apex.

and tapering it is *acuminate* (fig. 49).

d. Shape or General Outline.—The blade is subject to a great number of modifications in this respect, only the more important of which can be noticed here. Generally speaking, the two sides are more or less symmetrical, so that the leaf assumes some regular figure ; but in other instances it is more developed on one side than on the other, when the leaf is *unequal* or *oblique* (fig. 36). When the blade is narrow and nearly of the same breadth throughout the leaf is called *linear* (fig. 58, *l*); when broader at the centre and tapering towards both base and apex (fig. 5, *l*) it is *lanceolate ;* when longer than broad, and *oval* or *elliptical* in outline (figs. 37 and 47), it receives a corresponding name ; or if much longer than broad, and of the same oval shape, it is commonly termed *oblong.* When the blade resembles in shape the longitudinal section of an egg, the leaf is *ovate* or *egg-shaped* (figs. 36 and 39); or if of the same figure, but with the apex broader than the base (fig. 48), it is *obovate* or *inversely egg-shaped ;* when the leaf is generally more or less ovate, but hollowed out at the base into two rounded lobes, so that the blade resembles in shape the heart in a pack of cards, it is *cordate* or *heart-shaped* (fig. 49); or when hollowed out at the apex in a similar way, instead of at the base, it is *obcordate* or *inversely heart-shaped*, as in the seed leaves of the Radish (fig. 15). A leaf is *reniform* or *kidney-shaped* (fig. 50) when the blade resembles a kidney in shape ; it is *sagittate* or *arrow-shaped* (fig. 53) when it presents two acute lobes at its base pointing backwards; it is *hastate* or *halbert-shaped* (fig. 51) if the lobes at the base are placed horizontally ; or *auriculate* or *ear-shaped* (fig. 52) if, under the same circumstances, the lobes are separated from the blade. A leaf is *orbicular* or *round* when it

Fig. 49.

Fig. 49.—Cordate and acuminate leaf.

presents a round *outline;* or *sub-rotund* or *rounded* (fig. 27) when it approaches to that form. This term *sub* is frequently used as a prefix to other terms, in which case it means nearly approaching the modification to which it is prefixed, as sub-acute, nearly acute, &c.

Fig. 50.

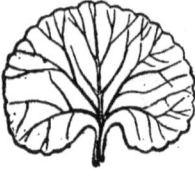

Fig. 51.

Fig. 52.

Fig. 50.—Leaf of Ground Ivy. Fig. 51. — Leaf of Sheep's Sorrel. Fig. 51.—Leaf of Bitter-sweet.

Fig. 53.

Fig 53.—Flowers and leaves of the common Arrow-head.

Leaves may also be frequently found intermediate in shape between two of those just described, in which case we use such terms as *ovate-lanceolate*, *linear-lanceolate*, &c., the application of which will be evident; but some experience is necessary before the young student will be able to apply them in practice, hence it is recommended that at first those leaves only which have a well-defined outline should be attended to.

e. Form.—By the form of a leaf we mean the solid configuration of the blade, that is, including its length, breadth, and thickness. These terms are therefore especially employed with thick or succulent leaves. Such leaves are described as *cylindrical, conical, needle-shaped, club-shaped, tubular, hood-shaped,* &c., in the same way as such terms are ordinarily applied, and hence need no special description here.

2. COMPOUND LEAVES.—A compound leaf has already been defined (page 44). Its leaflets are subject to similar modifications of shape, margin, &c., as the blades of simple leaves. Compound leaves are either *pinnate* or *palmate;* thus they are *pinnate* when the leaflets are arranged along the sides of the common petiole (fig. 54), and *palmate* when they all radiate from a common point (fig. 57).

a. Pinnate Leaves.—There are several varieties of pinnate leaves. Thus, when the leaf ends in an odd or single leaflet, it is *unequally pinnate* (fig. 59); when it terminates in a pair of leaflets, it is *abruptly or equally pinnate* (fig. 54), as in the Bitter Vetch; when the

Fig. 54.   Fig. 55.

Fig. 54.—Abruptly or equally pinnate leaf, Fig. 55.—Leaf of the Potato.

leaflets are alternately large and small, it is *interruptedly pinnate* (fig. 55); or when the terminal leaflet is the largest, and those below it gradually smaller, it is *lyrately pinnate.* The leaflets of a pinnate leaf are termed *pinnæ.*

When the partial petioles of a pinnate leaf bear leaflets along their sides, the leaf is said to be *bipinnate* (fig. 56), and the leaflets are termed *pinnules;* and when the pinnules become themselves pinnate, the leaf is *tripinnate.*

Fig. 56.   Fig. 57.

Fig. 56.—Bipinnate leaf of a species of *Gleditschia.* Fig. 57.—Biternate leaf.

b. Palmate or Digitate Leaves.—Such leaves are *unijugate* when there are only two leaflets; *trifoliate* or *ternate* when there are three (fig. 23, *r*); *quadrifoliate* when such a leaf has four leaflets; *quinquefoliate* or *quinate* when five; *septemfoliate* when seven; or *multifoliate* when more than seven. When the partial petioles of a ternate leaf are themselves trifoliate, the leaf is *biternate* (fig. 57), as in the Bane-berry; or when each of the divisions of a biternate leaf are themselves ternate, the leaf is said to be *triternate.* When compound leaves of the pinnate or palmate type are further divided than mentioned above, they are termed *decompound,*

B. Petiole or Leaf-Stalk.

The petiole is termed *simple* when undivided (figs. 39 and 54); or *compound* when divided into two or more portions, each of which bears a leaflet (fig. 57). In form the petiole is usually rounded below, and flattened, or more or less grooved, above; but in other cases it is cylindrical; or it becomes widened at its base, and surrounds the stem in the form of a sheath (fig. 58, *g*). In Grasses this sheath ends above in a membranous appendage, to which the name of *ligule* has been given (fig. 58, *lig*). Sometimes the petiole presents at its two edges a leaf-like border, when it is termed *winged*.

Fig. 58.

Fig. 58.—Portion of the stem of a Grass, with a leaf attached : *l*, blade; *lig*, ligule; *g*, sheathing petiole.

C. Stipules.

Stipules are liable to similar modifications of shape, margin, &c., as the blades and leaflets. When stipules are present, leaves are described as *stipulate;* or when absent, *exstipulate*. In rare cases the leaflets of a compound leaf have little stipules of their own, to which the name of *stipels* has been given, and the leaf is then termed *stipellate*. There are several kinds of stipules. Thus when they adhere to the petiole on each side they are said to be *adnate* (fig. 59, *s*); when quite

Fig. 59.

Fig. 59.—Leaf of Rose with stipules, *s*, at the base.

distinct from the petiole, they are *free* or *caulinary*
(fig. 6, *s*); when they form a sheath around the stem,
they are *ochreate* (fig. 5, *d*); and when, as in opposite
leaves, they are placed in the intervals between the
respective petioles on each side they are termed
interpetiolar.

4. ANOMALOUS OR IRREGULAR FORMS OF LEAVES.

Besides the forms of leaves already alluded to, there
are others of such an anomalous nature that they
require a special notice. In the first place, any part
of a leaf, like the branches of a stem, may acquire an
irregular development, and take the form of Spines
(fig. 40) and Tendrils, in which cases they receive
corresponding names. The most remarkable modifications of leaves are, however, *phyllodes* and *pitchers*.

The first are seen in their
most marked condition in
Australian Acacias (fig. 60).
In the leaves of these plants,
the hardened tissue of the
petiole, which under ordinary
circumstances remains as a
compact bundle until it reaches
the blade, begins to diverge as
soon as it leaves the stem or
branch, and its divisions become connected by soft tissue,
as in the ordinary blade of a
leaf; the petiole thus assuming
all the appearances of a lamina.
Such petioles have been termed
phyllodes; they may be generally distinguished from true
blades, amongst other characters, by being placed
nearly or quite in a vertical direction—that is, turn-
ing their margins instead of their surfaces to the
earth and heavens; and by their two surfaces being

Fig. 60.

Fig. 60.—A Leaf of an
Australian Acacia.

alike, whereas in true blades a manifest difference is commonly observable between the upper and lower surfaces.

The most anomalous of all the forms presented by leaves is that in which their parts become folded, so as to assume the shape of a pitcher, in which case they are called *pitcher-leaves* or *pitchers*. They may be well seen in the Pitcher plants (fig. 61), and Side-saddle plant.

Fig. 61.

Fig. 61.—Pitcher of a species of Pitcher Plant: *p*, pitcher, closed by the lid *l*.

QUESTIONS.

1. What is meant by appendages of the axis?
2. Arrange these appendages under the two heads of nutritive and reproductive.
3. Define a leaf, and show it varies in different plants by giving examples of such variation.
4. What is meant by the following terms :—node, internode, base, apex, margin, and axil?
5. What are deciduous and persistent leaves?
6. Explain the terms articulated and non-articulated.
7. What are the parts of a leaf?
8. What is meant by sessile and exstipulate leaves?
9. Which part of the leaf is generally most developed?
10. Define simple and compound leaves.

1. INSERTION AND ARRANGEMENT OF LEAVES.

11. What is meant by stalked or petiolate, and peltate or shield-shaped?
12. What is the difference between sessile, embracing or amplexicaul, and sheathing leaves?
13. Explain the terms decurrent, perfoliate, and connate.
14. What is meant by the terms alternate, opposite, and verticillate or whorled?
15. What is meant by a whorl or verticil, and the terms decussate, radical, and fascicle or tuft?
16. Explain the meaning of vernation.

2. SURFACE OF LEAVES.

17. What is meant by the term glabrous?
18. What are hairs and glands?
19. What are the usual forms of hairs?
20. What are scales or scurf, bristles, and prickles?
21. How is the surface of leaves, &c., modified by the varying abundance and character of hairs?
22. Describe the varying nature of glands, and explain the cause of the dots of certain leaves.
23. Describe the structure of a sting, and show how it produces its irritating effect.

3. PARTS OF LEAVES.

A. *Lamina or Blade.*

24. Explain the term venation.
25. Explain the terms midrib, ribs, veins, and veinlets.
26. Explain the terms pinnately-veined or feather-veined, and palmately-veined or radiate-veined.
27. What is meant by reticulated or netted, parallel, and forked venation?
28. What kind of venation is respectively found in dicotyledonous, monocotyledonous, and acotyledonous plants?
29. What is the difference between a simple and compound leaf?
30. Define the meaning of the terms leaflet, common petiole, and partial petiole?

1.—*Simple leaves.*

31. Explain the terms entire, serrate, dentate, crenate, wavy, and crisped.
32. Explain the terms biserrate, serrulate, bicrenate, crenulate, and doubly-toothed.
33. Explain what is meant by lobes and fissures, and define the terms cleft and bifid.
34. What are partitions and segments, and what is meant by the terms partite and sected?
35. Explain the meaning of the terms pinnatifid, pinnatipartite, and pinnatisected.
36. Explain the terms palmatifid, palmatipartite, and palmatisected.
37. What is the meaning of bipinnatifid?
38. Define the terms lyrate, runcinate, palmate, digitate, and pedate.
39. Explain the meaning of the terms obtuse, retuse, emarginate, truncate, mucronate, acute, and acuminate, as applied to the apex of leaves.
40. What is meant by an unequal or oblique leaf?
41. Explain the terms linear, lanceolate, oval or elliptical, and oblong.
42. Explain the terms ovate, obovate, cordate, obcordate, and reniform.
43. Explain the terms sagittate, hastate, auriculate, orbicular, and sub-rotund.

44. When is the term sub employed ?
45. Explain the terms ovate-lanceolate, and linear-lanceolate.
46. What is meant by the form of a leaf ? Distinguish between form and shape.
47. Explain the meaning attached to the terms conical and hood-shaped when applied to the forms of leaves.

2.—Compound leaves.

48. What are pinnate and palmate leaves ?
49. Explain the terms unequally pinnate, equally or abruptly pinnate, interruptedly pinnate, and lyrately pinnate.
50. What are pinnæ and pinnules ?
51. Explain the meaning of bipinnate and tripinnate.
52. Explain the terms unijugate, trifoliate or ternate, quadrifoliate, quinate, septemfoliate, and multifoliate.
53. What is meant by the terms biternate, triternate, and decompound ?

B. Petiole or Leaf-Stalk.

54. What is meant by a simple and compound petiole ?
55. What are the usual forms of the petiole ?
56. What is a ligule, and where is it found ?
57. What is a winged petiole ?

C. Stipules.

58. Distinguish between stipules and stipels.
59. Explain the terms stipulate, exstipulate, and stipellate.
60. What are adnate, caulinary, ochreate, and interpetiolar stipules ?

4. ANOMALOUS FORMS OF LEAVES.

61. What is meant by spiny leaves, and leaves with tendrils ?
62. What are phyllodes, and where are they found ?
63. How are phyllodes distinguished from the blades of leaves ?
64. What are pitchers or pitcher-leaves, and where are they found ?

CHAPTER III.

ORGANS OF REPRODUCTION.

Under this head we include the flower and its appendages. These are called Organs of Reproduction, because they have for their especial office the reproduction of the plant by the formation of seed.

SECTION I.—THE INFLORESCENCE.

The arrangement of the flowers upon the floral axis is termed the Inflorescence. We have under this head to describe—1st, The Bract or Floral Leaf; 2nd, The Floral Axis or Peduncle; and 3rd, The Kinds of Inflorescence.

1. BRACT OR FLORAL LEAF.

All leafy organs which are situated on the floral axis,

Fig. 62.

Fig. 63.

Fig. 62.—Plant of Toothwort: *b b*, bracts; *f f*, flowers. Fig. 63.—Cone of Stone Pine.

below the flowers are termed bracts, (fig. 62, *b b*). When bracts are present, the inflorescence is said to be *bracte-ated;* when they are absent, *ebracte-ated.* Bracts vary much in their nature and appearance, some being large and green like ordinary leaves, as in the white Dead-nettle, in which case they are termed *leafy bracts;* others *pi* hard and woody, **as in Fir-cones (fig. 63); and some** coloured, as in certain Arums; or membranous, or presenting other peculiarities.

Varieties of Bracts.—Certain varieties of arrangement and

Fig. 64.

Fig. 64. — Narrow-leaved Water Parsnip *gi*, general involucre surrounding the general umbel; *pi*, partial involucre, or involucre around a partial umbel.

forms of bracts have received special names, the more important of which are as follows:—thus, when one or more circles or whorls of bracts are placed around one flower (fig. 78, *b*), or a number of flowers (figs. 29, *b*, and 44, *i*), this arrangement of bracts is termed an involucre. In the true involucre the constituent bracts are distinct from one another; but when they grow together at their base, as in the cup of the Acorn (fig. 66), they then form what is called a *cupule*. When a bract is of large size and sheathing, so as to surround and completely enclose the flowers in a young state, it is called a *spathe*. This is well seen in Arums (fig. 65, *b*), and in Palms (fig. 67, *b*). In the latter

Fig 65. Fig. 66

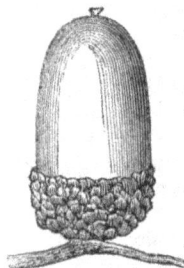

b

Fig. 65.—Flowers and leaves of the Cuckoo-pint: *b*, spathe. Fig. 66.—Fruit of the Oak, surrounded by a cupule.

plants the spathes are sometimes as much as twenty feet in length, and enclose as many as 200,000 flowers. The bracts of Grasses and Sedges, which are found at the base of each partial inflorescence, termed a *locusta* or *spikelet* (fig. 72, *gl*), are called *glumes*.

2. THE PEDUNCLE OR FLOWER-STALK.

The term peduncle is applied to the stalk of a solitary flower (68), or to one which bears a number of

Fig. 67.   Fig. 68.

Fig. 67.—Palm flowers surrounded by spathe, *b*. Fig. 68.—Plant of Snowdrop.

sessile flowers (fig. 69); or if the floral axis branches all is called a *peduncle* (fig. 7, *p*), with the exception of the stalks immediately supporting the individual flowers, which are termed *pedicels* (fig. 7, *ped*). When a peduncle is elongated in a longitudinal direction, and gives off flowers, or branches bearing flowers along its sides, it is called the *rachis* (figs. 69 and 73); but

Fig. 69.

when shortened and dilated more or less horizontally, and bearing numerous flowers, it is termed a *receptacle* (fig. 44, *r*). When plants have no aerial stem bearing leaves, the peduncle, which then necessarily arises, at or under the ground, is called a *Scape* or *radical peduncle* (figs. 26 and 68); when the peduncle becomes flattened and assumes the form of a phyllode, it is called a *phylloid peduncle* or *pedicel*.

3. KINDS OF INFLORESCENCE.

There are several kinds of inflorescence, all the regular of which may be arranged in two great divisions, which are respectively termed *Indefinite* or *Indeterminate*, and *Definite* or *Determinate*. In the former, the main or primary axis is terminated by a growing point, and hence such an axis has the power of growing in an upward direction or of dilating more or less horizontally, in the same way as the terminal bud of a stem or branch has the power of elongating, and thus adding to its length; there is, consequently, no necessary limit

Fig 69.—Inflorescence of Broom-rape.

to the growth of such an axis, and hence the name of Indeterminate or Indefinite which is applied to it. Such an inflorescence is also termed *axillary*, because as the axis grows upwards it continues to develop on its sides flowers from the axil of bracts. In the *Definite* or *Determinate Inflorescence*, on the contrary, the primary axis is terminated at an early age by the production of a flower; such an axis has, therefore, a limit at once put to its growth, and hence the names of *Definite*, *Determinate*, or *Terminal* applied to it. Each of these divisions of inflorescence presents us with several modifications, the more important of which we now proceed to describe.

1. INDETERMINATE INFLORESCENCE. — The simplest kind of inflorescence in this class is that in which solitary flowers are developed in the axils of leaves or bracts; the flowers are then said to be *solitary* and *axillary*. When a number of flowers instead of one are developed, a number of kinds of inflorescence arise,

Fig. 70. Fig. 71.

Fig 70.—Staminate catkin of a Willow. Fig. 71.—Pistillate catkin of a Willow.

and in all such inflorescences it will be necessarily found

from their mode of growth that the lower or outer flower-buds will open first because such buds are the oldest, and that the order of expansion will proceed in succession from the base to the apex if the axis be elongated (figs. 24 and 69), or from the circumference towards the centre if the axis be depressed or dilated (fig. 74). Such a mode of opening is therefore called *centripetal.*

The principal kinds of indeterminate inflorescence are as follows:—

a. The Spike. —In this the primary axis is elongated and bears sessile flowers on its sides (fig. 69). There are several modifications of the spike; thus the *amentum* or *catkin* is a kind of spike which bears only barren flowers— that is, only staminate (fig. 70) or pistillate (fig. 71) ones ; the *spadix* (figs. 65 and 67) is a spike with a succulent axis, in which the separate flowers have no special bracts, but the whole commonly enclosed

Fig. 72.* Fig. 73.

gl

Fig. 72.—Inflorescence of Barley, the glumes, *gl,* end in long bristles. Fig. 73.—Panicled inflorescence of a Grass.

in a spathe; and *locusta* or *spikelet* is the name given to the partial inflorescence of Grasses (fig. 72) and Sedges. The peculiarity of this latter is that the spike has only a few flowers, and these without floral envelopes, and the whole having at the base one or two bracts called glumes (fig. 72, *gl*).

b. The Raceme.—In this form the primary axis is elongated, and bears flowers placed on pedicels of nearly equal length (figs. 24 and 62).

c. The Corymb.—This is a kind of raceme in which the lower pedicels are longer than those towards and at the apex, so that the whole forms a somewhat level top.

d. The Panicle.—This is a more branched form of inflorescence than the raceme—that is to say, one in which the stalks springing from the primary axis do not immediately bear flowers, but give off branches on which the flowers are placed (fig. 73).

e. The Capitulum or *Head.*—This is formed by a number of sessile flowers crowded together on a receptacle, and the whole being surrounded by an involucre (figs. 44, *f*, and 74).

f. The Umbel.—This is a kind of inflorescence in which the primary axis gives off from its apex a number of pedicels of nearly equal length, radiating from each other like the ribs of an umbrella, and each bearing a flower (fig. 30, *a*).

Fig. 74.

Fig. 74.—Capitulum of Scabious. The outermost flowers (florets) may be seen to be more expanded than the inner.

When the branches (pedicels) of the primary axis, instead of directly bearing flowers, themselves divide in an umbellate manner, a *compound umbel* is formed (fig. 64). In this case the primary umbel is called the *general umbel*, and the others formed by the divisions of this, *umbellules* or *partial umbels*. In like manner, when the general umbel is surrounded by an involucre, this is called a *general involucre* (fig. 64, *gi*), and if similar arrangements of bracts are placed around the partial umbels, each of these is termed an *involucel* or *partial involucre, p i*.

2. DETERMINATE INFLORESCENCE.—When the primary axis only bears a solitary flower at its apex which terminates its growth, this is called a *solitary terminal flower;* but if other flowers are produced, we have other kinds of inflorescence, all of which are necessarily characterised, from their mode of growth, by the terminal or central flowers of each axis opening first, as such flowers are the oldest, and the order of expansion proceeding in succession from above downwards, or from within outwards (fig. 81). Such an order of expansion is called *centrifugal* or *cymose.*

The general name of *cyme* is applied to all such inflorescences, and they are further distinguished as

Fig. 75.

Fig. 75.—Helicoid cyme of a species of *Myosotis.*

two-branched (dichotomous), or *three-branched (trichoto-mous)*, according to the number of their branches ; or still better as *corymbose, umbellate, spiked, racemose*, or *panicled*, from their resemblance, except in the order of expansion of their flowers, to the ordinary kinds of indeterminate inflorescence thus named.

Other kinds of cymes have received special names, thus *helicoid* or *scorpioid cyme* is applied when the upper part of the axis is coiled up in a circinate manner, like a scorpion's tail (fig. 75) ; the term *fascicle* is given to a cyme when the flowers, which are placed on short stalks of nearly equal length, are somewhat crowded together ; and *glomerule* to a cyme with sessile or nearly sessile flowers collected into a more or less rounded head.

QUESTIONS.

1. What is an organ of reproduction ?
2. What is meant by the inflorescence ?

1. BRACT OR FLORAL LEAF.

3. Define a bract, and explain the terms bracteated and ebracteated.
4. Explain the term leafy bract, and give examples of other variations of bracts in nature and appearance.
5. Define the following varieties of bracts : involucre, cupule, spathe, and glume.

2. PEDUNCLE OR FLOWER-STALK.

6. What are peduncles and pedicels ?
7. Define a rachis, receptacle, radical peduncle, and phylloid peduncle.

3. KINDS OF INFLORESCENCE.

8. What do you understand by the term Indefinite, Indeterminate, or Axillary Inflorescence ?
9. What do you understand by the term Definite, Determinate, or Terminal Inflorescence ?
10. What is meant by a solitary and axillary inflorescence ?
11. Explain the meaning of the term centripetal.
12. Define a spike, amentum or catkin, spadix, and locusta or spikelet.
13. Define a raceme.
14. Define a corymb.
15. Define a panicle.
16. What is a capitulum or head ?

17. What is an umbel?   Distinguish between a simple and compound umbel.

18. What is meant by the terms general umbel, partial umbel or umbellule, general involucre, and partial involucre or involucel?

19. What is meant by a solitary terminal flower?

20. Explain the meaning of centrifugal or cymose order of expansion.

21. What is meant by a cyme, and what are dichotomous and trichotomous cymes?

22. What do you understand by corymbose, umbellate, spiked, panicled, and racemose cymes?

23. Define a helicoid or scorpioid cyme.

24. What is a fascicle or fascicled cyme?

25. Define a glomerule.

SECTION II.—OF THE PARTS OF THE FLOWER.

The parts of a flower have already been treated of in a general manner (see page 14), and we now pass to describe them more in detail.

1. THE FLORAL ENVELOPES.

A. THE CALYX.

We have already defined the calyx as the outermost envelope of the flower, and composed of one or more, usually green, leafy organs, termed sepals.   In many flowers, of which the Fuchsia may be taken as an example, the sepals are coloured, instead of being green, in which case the calyx is said to be *petaloid*.   This term is only commonly applied in dicotyledonous plants; for, as already mentioned, the two floral envelopes are usually coloured in monocotyledonous plants, and the term *perianth* then used to indicate the two whorls taken collectively.

The sepals, as regards their outline, margin, apex, &c., are characterised by similar terms as applied to the blades of leaves.   They vary in their direction, being *erect* or turned upwards; *connivent* or turned inwards; *divergent* or *patulous* when spreading outwards; and *reflexed* when their ends are turned downwards.

The sepals are either distinct from each other, or

more or less united into one body. In the first case
the calyx is commonly described as *polysepalous*, in the
latter *monosepalous;* the latter term is, however, incor-
rect, as it implies that the calyx has only one sepal,
and hence many botanists use instead the more correct
term of *gamosepalous*, which simply implies that the
sepals are united.

1. POLYSEPALOUS CALYX.—A polysepalous calyx is
called *regular* if it consists of sepals of equal size and
like form, arranged in a symmetrical manner (fig. 9);
and it is said to be *irregular* when these conditions are
not complied with (fig. 77). It is further described as
consisting of two, three, four, or more sepals, according
to their number.

2. MONOSEPALOUS OR GAMOSEPALOUS CALYX.—Various degrees of union take place in the constituent
sepals of a monosepalous calyx, and different terms are
used accordingly to indicate that degree ; thus, if the
union is complete, the calyx is *entire;* if the sepals are
united nearly to the top, it is *toothed;* if only attached
at the base, *partite;* or if about to the middle, *cleft* or
fissured, and the number of teeth, partitions, or fissures
indicated by the prefix of numerals. When the union
exists in any marked degree, the part where the sepals
are united is called the *tube*, the free portion the *limb*,
and the orifice of the tube the *throat*.

If the union be unequal between the sepals, or the
parts are of different sizes, or of irregular forms, the
calyx is *irregular;* if, on the contrary, the parts are
alike in form, of the same size, and united in a symmetrical manner, the calyx is *regular*. In the latter
case the calyx is described as *tubular, bell-shaped,
conical*, &c., in like manner as the corolla is so
designated (see page 74).

The normal position of the calyx is to be free or
quite distinct from the wall of the ovary (fig. 9), in
which case it is said to be *inferior* or *non-adherent*,
and the ovary is described as *superior ;* but in other
cases the tube of a monosepalous calyx, or of a perianth,

adheres more or less to the ovary, when the ovary is said to be *inferior* (fig. 76, *o*), and the calyx *superior* or *adherent*.

In the latter case the limb presents various modifications; thus it may be *petaloid*, *foliaceous*, *membranous*, which terms are readily understood; or it may be altogether absent, when it is described as *obsolete*. In other instances the limb of the calyx is only developed in the form of bristles, hairs, or feathery processes, when it is said to be *pappose* (fig. 44, *p*).

Fig. 77.

Fig. 76.

Fig. 76.—Vertical section of the flower of a Myrtle: *cal,* tube of the calyx adherent to the ovary, *o*; *s,* stamens. Fig. 77.—Figure of Larkspur: *sp,* spurred calyx.

APPENDAGES OF THE CALYX.—When the tube of a monosepalous calyx or a sepal bulges out at the base into a little sac, the term *gibbous* or *saccate* is used (fig. 80, *c*); or if the calyx has one or more tubular prolongations downwards, it is *spurred* (fig. 77, *sp*), and each prolonged portion is called a *spur*.

DURATION OF THE CALYX.—The duration of the calyx varies; thus, when it falls off as the flower expands, it is *caducous;* when about the same time as the corolla, it is *deciduous;* when it remains after the flowering is over, it is *persistent;* if under similar circumstances it presents a shrivelled appearance, *marcescent;* or when it is persistent, and continues to grow, it is *accrescent.*

QUESTIONS.

1. What is meant by the term petaloid as applied to the calyx ?

2. Explain the terms erect, connivent, divergent or patulous, and reflexed.

3. What is meant by a polysepalous, monosepalous, and gamosepalous calyx ?

4. What do you understand by a regular and irregular polysepalous calyx ?

5. Explain the terms entire, toothed, partite, and cleft or fissured, as applied to a monosepalous calyx.

6. What is meant by the tube, limb, and throat of a monosepalous calyx ?

7. Explain the terms regular and irregular as applied to a monosepalous calyx.

8. What is meant by an inferior, and what by a superior calyx ?

9. Explain the terms petaloid, foliaceous, membranous, and obsolete as applied to the limb of the calyx.

10. What is meant by a pappose calyx ?

11. Define the terms gibbous or saccate, and spurred.

12. Explain the terms caducous, deciduous, persistent, marcescent, and accrescent, as applied to the duration of the calyx.

B. THE COROLLA.

The corolla is the inner floral envelope ; its parts are called petals. It is usually the most showy and conspicuous part of the flower, and what in common language is termed the flower. In some cases, however, the corolla is green like the calyx. Petals are frequently narrowed below into a stalk-like portion (fig. 79, *o*). The narrowed portion is then termed the *claw* or *unguis,* and the broad portion the *limb,* and the petal is said to be *unguiculate* or *clawed.*

The petals are subject to various modifications of outline, margin, direction, &c., which are described by

Fig. 78.

Fig. 79.

Fig. 78.—Caryophyllaceous corolla: *b*, bracts; *c*, calyx; *p p*, petals; *e*, stamens. Fig. 79.—One of the petals of Fig. 78: *ò*, claw or unguis; *l*, limb, which is fringed at the margin.

similar terms as are employed in like modifications of the sepals and leaves.

The petals, like the sepals, may be either distinct, or more or less united into one body. In the former case the corolla is said to be *polypetalous;* in the latter, *monopetalous* or *gamopetalous.*

1. POLYPETALOUS COROLLA.—The corolla is termed *regular* and *irregular* in the same sense as already described (page 69) with the polysepalous calyx. The number of petals is also indicated by the prefix of numerals

Fig. 80.

Fig. 80.—Cruciate Corolla : *c*, gibbous calyx.

as with the sepals. Some forms of both regular and irregular polypetalous corollas have received special names as follows :—

A. Regular Polypetalous Corollas.—Of these there are three forms to be alluded to.

1. *Cruciform* or *Cruciate.*—This is composed of four petals, usually with claws, although not necessarily, and arranged in the form of a Maltese cross (fig. 80).

2. *Caryophyllaceous.*—This is composed of five petals, with long claws enclosed in the tube of the calyx, and their limbs placed at right angles to the claws (figs. 78 and 79).

3. *Rosaceous.*—This consists of five petals without claws, or with very short ones, and spreading in a regular manner (fig. 81).

B. Irregular Polypetalous Corollas.—There is only one form of such corollas which requires any particular description, namely :—

The Papilionaceous.—This derives its name from the fancied resemblance which it bears to a butterfly (fig. 82). It is composed of five petals, one of which,

Fig. 81. Fig. 82.

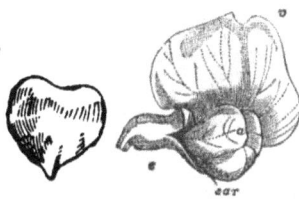

Fig. 81.—Rosaceous corolla, with one of the petals of the same placed at the right hand side. Fig. 82.—Papilionaceous corolla: *c*, calyx; *v*, standard; *car*, carina or keel; *a*, wings.

being placed at the upper part of the flower, is termed the *standard, v ;* two are inferior, and more or less united, so as to form a somewhat boat-shaped cavity, called the *keel, car ;* and two lateral, called the *wings* or *alæ, a.*

2. MONOPETALOUS OR GAMOPETALOUS COROLLA.—The petals, like the sepals, are united in varying degrees, which are characterised by similar terms ; and such a corolla may be regular or irregular, as described in speaking of a monosepalous calyx. The special forms are as follows :—

A. Regular Monopetalous Corollas.—Of these the more important are—

1. *Tubular*, where the form is nearly cylindrical throughout, the limb not spreading.

2. *Campanulate* or *Bell-shaped*, where the corolla resembles a bell in form (fig. 7, *f*).

3. *Funnel-shaped*, where the form is that of an inverted cone, like a funnel.

4. *Salver-shaped*, when the tube is long and narrow, and the limb at right angles to it (fig. 83).

5. *Rotate* or *Wheel-shaped*, having a short tube and flat spreading limb.

6. *Urceolate*, when the tube is swollen in the middle and contracted at both the base and apex (fig. 84).

Fig. 83.   Fig. 84.   Fig. 85.   Fig. 86.

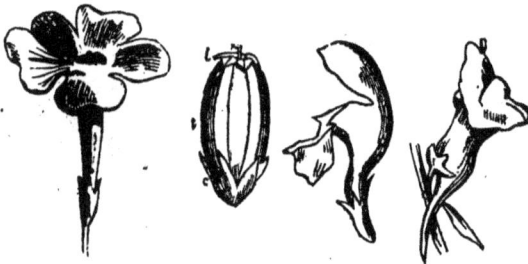

Fig. 83.—Salver-shaped corolla. Fig. 84.—Flower of a Heath *c*, calyx; *t*, *l*, Urceolate corolla. Fig. 85.—Labiate corolla of the Dead-nettle. Fig. 86.—Personate corolla of the Toadflax, spurred at the base.

B. Irregular Monopetalous Corollas.—The principal are the *labiate, personate,* and *ligulate.*

1. *Labiate.*—This is a kind of corolla in which the limb is divided into two portions, called lips, which are placed posteriorly and anteriorly, the former overhanging the latter, and each portion so arranged as not to close the throat or orifice of the tube (fig. 85). When the upper lip is much arched, this form of labiate corolla is termed *ringent* or *gaping.*

2. *Personate* or *Masked.*—This is essentially a labiate

corolla, but distinguished by its lower lip forming a projection, called the *palate*, against the upper lip, so as to close the throat (fig. 86).

8. *Ligulate* or *Strap-shaped*.—If what would be otherwise a tubular corolla is split open on one side, so as to become flattened above like a strap (fig. 87), it is called *ligulate* or *strap-shaped*.

Fig. 87.   Fig. 88.   Fig. 89.

Fig. 87.—Ligulate corolla. Fig. 88.—Flower of Valerian: *c*, *l*, calyx adherent to the ovary; *g*, gibbous corolla. Fig. 89.—Flower of Narcissus: *b*, bract; *o*, ovary; *c*, perianth, with a corona on the inner surface.

ANOMALOUS FORMS AND APPENDAGES OF PETALS.—One or more of the petals of a monopetalous or polypetalous corolla may be *gibbous* or *saccate* (fig. 88, *g*) or *spurred* (fig. 86), in a similar way to the sepals.

On the inner surface of petals, commonly at the junction of the claw and limb, we may frequently find

appendages in the form of scales or hair-like processes of various natures. Sometimes these scales
become more or less united, and form a cup-shaped
process (fig. 89, *c*), to which the term *corona* is applied,
and the corolla is then said to be *crowned*. Many of
these appendages were formerly described as *nectaries*,
although few possess the power of secreting the honey-
like matter or nectar from which they derived their
names.

DURATION OF THE COROLLA.—The corolla is generally
more fugitive than the calyx, although its duration
varies. The terms *caducous, deciduous, persistent*, and
marcescent, are applied to it in the same sense as with
the calyx.

QUESTIONS.

1. What is the corolla?
2. Explain the terms claw or unguis, and limb as applied to a petal, and describe what is meant by an unguiculate petal.
3. What is meant by polypetalous, monopetalous, and gamo-petalous corollas?
4. Explain the terms regular and irregular as applied to a poly-petalous corolla.
5. Define a cruciform or cruciate corolla.
6. What is meant by a caryophyllaceous corolla?
7. What is meant by a rosaceous corolla?
8. What is a papilionaceous corolla?
9. Define the standard, keel, and wings of a papilionaceous corolla.
10. Explain the terms entire, toothed, regular, and irregular as applied to a monopetalous corolla.
11. What is a tubular corolla?
12. What is a campanulate corolla?
13. What is a funnel-shaped corolla?
14. What is a salver-shaped corolla?
15. What is a rotate corolla?
16. What is an urceolate corolla?
17. Define a labiate, and a ringent or gaping corolla.
18. What is a personate or masked corolla?
19. What is a ligulate corolla?
20. What are gibbous or saccate, and spurred petals or corollas?
21. What are the scales of petals?
22. What is a corona, and what is meant by the term crowned?
23. What are nectaries?
24. Explain the terms caducous, deciduous, persistent, and mar-cescent, as applied to the duration of the corolla.

2. The Essential Organs of Reproduction.

The essential organs of reproduction are the andrœcium and gynœcium, which together form the two inner whorls of the flower.   Flowers usually possess both these organs, and are hence termed *bisexual;* when one only is present, they are *unisexual*, and then described as staminate or pistillate, as already noticed (page 17). In some cases a flower has neither andrœcium or gynœcium, when it is described as *neuter*.   When flowers are unisexual, both staminate and pistillate flowers may be borne on the same plant, in which case it is said to be *monœcious;* or upon different plants of the same species, when it is *diœcious*.

A. The Andrœcium or Staminal Whorl.

The andrœcium is the whorl or whorls of organs situated next the corolla on the inside, and it is so called because it forms the male system of flowering plants. The parts of which it is composed are termed *stamens,* each of which (fig. 11), in its perfect condition, consists of a thread-like stalk or *filament*, and of a little bag or case called the *anther*, which contains a powdery matter or *pollen*.   When the pollen is absent, as is rarely the case, the anther is described as *sterile;* and when the filament is absent, the anther is said to be *sessile*.

1. The Filament.—The filament varies in form, length, colour, direction, duration, &c., the terms expressive of which need no special description.

2. The Anther.—The anther usually consists of two parallel lobes separated by a portion called the *connective,* to which the filament is attached.   Each of these lobes has a cavity in its interior called a *cell,* and hence anthers are commonly two-celled, but occasionally they are one-celled, and rarely four-celled.   That surface of the anther to which the filament and ·connective are attached is called the *back*, and the opposite surface is the *face;* this may be distinguished from the back by its more or less grooved appearance.   The face is generally turned

towards the pistil or centre of the flower, in which case the anther is *introrse;* but in some flowers it is directed towards the petals or circumference of the flower, when it is said to be *extrorse.*

The mode of attachment of the anther to the filament varies in different flowers. Thus, the anther is sometimes attached throughout its whole length to the filament, when it is said to be *adnate;* in other cases the filament is firmly fixed to its base, when it is *innate;* or it is only attached by a point to the back of the anther, which swings upon it, when it is *versatile.*

In form and colour, &c., the anther and its lobes are subject to numerous modifications, but these need no special description.

Dehiscence of the Anther.—When ripe, the face of the anther opens, and the contained pollen is discharged; this act is called the *dehiscence* of the anther, and may take place by the opening of each lobe in a longitudinal direction from the base to the apex (fig. 11), when it is called *longitudinal;* or in a transverse or horizontal direction, and then termed *transverse* dehiscence; or simply by pores or slits at different points of the anther, when it is called *porous;* or the whole or portions of the face of the anther open like trap-doors, which are attached at the top, and turn back as if on a hinge (fig. 12, *a*), when the term *valvular* dehiscence is applied.

THE STAMENS GENERALLY.—Having now described the two parts of a stamen we have, in the next place, to take a general view of the stamens as regards their relations to one another, and to the other parts of the flower. This may be treated of under four heads, as follows:—

1. *Number.*—The stamens may be equal or unequal in number to the sepals and petals, and corresponding terms are used accordingly. The actual number of stamens a flower contains is indicated by the Greek numerals prefixed to the word *androus,* which means male or stamen. Thus a flower having one stamen is

monandrous; two, *diandrous* (fig. 10); three, *triandrous;* four, *tetrandrous,* and so on. When the stamens are few in number, so as to be readily counted, they are said to be *definite,* when more than twenty in number, *indefinite.*

2. *Insertion or Position.*—When the stamens are free from the calyx and pistil, and arise directly from the thalamus below the latter organ (fig. 90), they are said to be *hypogynous,* which signifies under the female or pistil. When the stamens are attached to the corolla, they are *epipetalous;* when they adhere to the calyx more or less, so that their position becomes somewhat lateral to the pistil instead of below it, they are said to be *perigynous.* When the calyx is adherent to the ovary so that it appears to arise from its apex, the intermediate corolla and stamens are also necessarily placed on the summit of the ovary, and are then called *epigynous* (fig. 76). In some flowers the stamens not only

Fig. 90.

Fig. 90.—Stamens arising below the pistil in a species of *Ranunculus: c,* carpels; *st,* stamens.

adhere to the ovary, but the upper part of the stamens and pistil become completely united also, and thus form a column in the centre of the flower, in which case the flower is said to be *gynandrous.*

3. *Union.*—The stamens may be either perfectly distinct from each other; or union may take place between them either by their anthers or by their filaments, or by both anthers and filaments. Various terms are employed to indicate the union of the parts of the stamens; thus when the anthers cohere the stamens are termed *syngenesious.* When the filaments unite the union may take place in one or more bundles, the number being indicated by a Greek numeral prefixed to the word *adelphous,* signifying *brotherhood;* thus, when in one bundle, the stamens are *monadelphous;* in two, *diadelphous;* in three, *triadelphous;* and when in more than three, *polyadelphous,* or the latter term is used in

all cases when the stamens are united in more than two bundles.

4. *Relative Length.*—When the stamens are shorter than the tube of the corolla, so as to be enclosed within it (figs. 83 and 84), they are described as *included;* or when longer, so as to extend beyond it, they are said to be *exserted* (fig. 88). As regards themselves, the stamens may be as nearly as possible of the same length, or more or less unequal; in the latter case, there is sometimes a definite relation existing between the stamens as to their length, and certain names are applied to indicate such forms of regularity. Thus, when there are six stamens to the flower, of which four are long and arranged in pairs opposite to each other, and alternating with two shorter solitary stamens, we apply the term *tetradynamous* to indicate such an arrangement; or when there are but four stamens, two of which are long and two short, they are said to be *didynamous.*

In the once celebrated Linnæan System, the characters of no less than twenty out of the twenty-four classes which that system comprised were derived from the number, position, union, and relative length of the stamens.

QUESTIONS.

1. What do you understand by bisexual, unisexual, staminate, pistillate, and neuter flowers?
2. Explain the terms monœcious and diœcious.

A. *The Andrœcium.*

3. What is meant by the Andrœcium?
4. What are stamens, and what are the parts of a stamen?
5. What is meant by sterile and sessile anthers?
6. Is the filament liable to variation?
7. What is the structure of the anther?
8. Explain the terms face, back, introrse, and extrorse, as applied to the anther.
9. Explain the terms adnate, innate, and versatile.
10. What is meant by the dehiscence of the anther?
11. What do you understand by longitudinal, transverse, porous, and valvular dehiscence of anthers?
12. In what respects do stamens vary in number, and how is the number indicated?

13. Explain the terms monandrous, tetrandrous, definite, and indefinite.

14. Explain the terms hypogynous, epipetalous, perigynous, and epigynous.

15. What is the meaning of the term gynandrous?

16. Explain the term syngenesious.

17. Explain the meaning of adelphous, and describe what is meant by monadelphous, diadelphous, and polyadelphous.

18. What is meant by included and exserted stamens?

19. Explain the meaning of the terms tetradynamous and didynamous.

20. What were the characters of most of the classes of the Linnæan System derived from?

B. THE GYNŒCIUM OR PISTIL.

The pistil is the terminal or central organ of the flower; it is called the gynœcium because it represents the female system in flowering plants. It consists of one or more parts called *carpels*, which are either distinct from each other (fig. 90, *c*), or combined into one body (figs. 8 and 9). The pistil is *simple* when there is but one carpel (fig. 12), and *compound* when there are more carpels than one (figs. 8 and 9). Each carpel (fig. 12), as already noticed, consists—first, of a hollow inferior portion, which arises from the thalamus, and is called the *ovary*, and which contains in its interior one or more little bodies called *ovules*, which ultimately become the seeds, and which are attached to a projection on the walls termed the *placenta*; and, second, of a *stigma*, or space of variable size, which is either placed directly on the ovary, when it is said to be *sessile*, or it is raised on a stalk prolonged from the ovary, called the *style*. The terms ovary, style, and stigma are applied in precisely the same sense when speaking of a compound pistil, in which the parts are completely united, as with the simple carpel.

THE GYNŒCIUM GENERALLY.—Having now alluded to the parts of the carpel, we have in the next place to refer briefly to the gynœcium or pistil generally. The carpels, as just noticed, when there are more than one, may be either distinct from each other or more or less united;

in the former case the pistil is said to be *apocarpous* (fig. 90), in the latter *syncarpous* (figs. 8 and 9). When the pistil is apocarpous the number of component carpels is indicated by the prefix of a Greek numeral to the termination *gynous*, which means female, and the flower receives corresponding names accordingly. In a syncarpous pistil the number of styles is also indicated in a similar way. Thus, a flower with one carpel or one style is *monogynous*, with two carpels or two styles *digynous*, with three carpels or three styles *trigynous*, and so on.

In a syncarpous pistil the union of the carpels may be either partial or complete; thus, either by their stigmas only, or more or less by their styles, or far more frequently in various degrees by their ovaries. In the latter case, when the ovaries of two or more adjoining carpels are completely united the body thus formed is called a *compound ovary*. A compound ovary may either have as many cavities as there are component ovaries, or it may only have one cavity; and as these differences have an important bearing upon the position of the placenta or point of attachment of the ovules, it is necessary that we should now describe the causes of such differences. Thus, in the first place, suppose we have three carpels placed side by side (fig. 91, *a*); each of these will possess a single cavity corresponding to its constituent ovary, and separated from the cavities of adjoining carpels by a

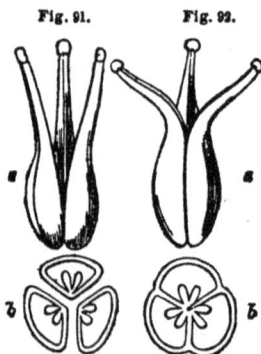

Fig. 91.—*a*, Diagram of three carpels placed side by side; *b*, a transverse section of the ovaries of the same. Fig. 92.—*a*, Diagram of three ovaries united by their ovaries, the styles being free; *b*, a transverse section of the ovaries of the same.

double wall, one-half being formed by the side of its own ovary and the other by that of the one next to it. This will be best seen on making a transverse section of the whole (fig. 91, *b*). Now suppose that these three carpels, instead of being distinct, were united by their ovaries (fig. 92, *a*) so as to form a compound ovary, the latter must necessarily have also as many cavities as there are component carpels (fig. 92, *b*), and each cavity would be separated from adjoining cavities by a wall, which is called a *dissepiment* or *partition*, and which is formed by the united sides of the two adjoining ovaries.

The cavities thus formed in the ovary are called *cells*, and such an ovary would therefore be termed *three-celled*; or if formed of two, four, five, or many carpels, it would be *two-celled, four-celled, five-celled,* or *many-celled*.

In the second case, when a compound ovary has but one cavity, it is formed by the ovaries of its constituent carpels remaining flattened open bodies, which become united by their contiguous margins; or by the union of ovaries partially folded inwards, so that all their cavities communicate in the centre (fig. 93), and hence in reality one-celled.

PLACENTATION.—We are now in a position to under-stand the different kinds of placentation. The term *placenta* is applied to the more or less marked projection in the cavity of the ovary to which the ovule or ovules are attached; and by *placentation* we mean the manner in which the placentas are distributed, which varies in different plants, but is always the same for any particular species.

In the simple ovary, or that formed out of one carpel, the placenta is always situated at what is termed the ventral suture or the inner margin of the ovary; such a placenta is therefore commonly termed *marginal* (fig. 12).

In compound ovaries we have three kinds of placentation, namely, *axile* or *central, parietal,* and *free central.* The *axile* (fig. 92, *b*) occurs in all compound ovaries with more than one cell, because in these each of the ovaries of which it is composed is placed in a similar position to that of the simple ovary, and hence the placentas situated at their inner margins must be arranged in the centre or axis.

In a compound one-celled ovary there are two kinds of placentation—the *parietal* and the *free central*. The placenta-

Fig. 93.   Fig. 94.

tion is termed *parietal* when the ovules are attached to placentas either placed directly on the inner wall of the ovary, or upon incomplete dissepiments formed (as already noticed) by the partially in-folded ovaries (fig. 93, *pl*); and a *free central placenta* is produced when the placentas are situated in the centre of the ovary, and perfectly unconnected with the wall (fig. 94, *p*).

Fig. 93.—Tranverse section of the one-celled ovary of an Orchis: *c*, carpels, with their margins slightly infolded; *pl*, placentas. Fig. 94.—Vertical section of the ovary of a species of Chickweed: *o*, ovary; *p*, free central placenta; *g*, ovules; *s*, styles.

QUESTIONS.

1. What is the gynœcium, and why is it so called ?
2. What is a carpel ?
3. What is meant by a simple and compound pistil ?
4. Mention and describe the parts of a carpel.
5. What is a sessile stigma ?
6. Explain the terms apocarpous and syncarpous.
7. How do we indicate the number of carpels in a compound pistil ?
8. What is meant by a compound ovary ?
9. In what way does the compound ovary vary in respect to the number of its cavities ?

10. Explain how a compound ovary with three cavities is formed.

11. What are dissepiments and cells?

12. Explain how a compound ovary with one cavity or cell is produced.

13. What is meant by the terms placenta and placentation?

14. What is meant by a marginal placenta, and where does it occur?

15. What is meant by axile or central placentation?

16. What is meant by parietal placentation?

17. What is meant by a free central placenta?

SECTION III.—THE FRUIT AND SEED.

1. THE FRUIT.

Nature and Characters of the Fruit.—After the process of fertilization has been effected (see page 17), important changes take place in the pistil and surrounding organs of the flower, the result of which is the formation of the fruit. The fruit consists essentially of the mature ovary or ovaries, containing the impregnated ovule or ovules, which are then termed seeds. Even the styles and stigmas mostly disappear, but the remains of the style frequently exist in the form of a little point on the fruit, which is then commonly described as *apiculate*, and in this way small fruits may be generally distinguished from seeds.

Although the fruit thus consists essentially of the mature ovary or ovaries, other parts of the flower also frequently enter into its composition. Thus in those cases where the calyx is adherent to the ovary, as in the Apple and Gooseberry, it necessarily forms part of the fruit; in the Strawberry the fruit consists of the succulent thalamus bearing the carpels, commonly called seeds, on its convex surface; in the Acorn and Filbert the fruit consists of pistil, calyx, and bracts, combined together; in the Pine-apple it is composed of the ovaries, floral envelopes, and bracts of several flowers; and in the Fig we have also a fruit formed of a number of

separate flowers enclosed in an enlarged fleshy receptacle. These examples will show the varying nature of
the fruit, so that although it consists essentially of the
mature ovary, the term is also applied to whatever is
combined with that ovary, so as to form a covering to
the seeds.

As the fruit is formed essentially out of the ovary,
the modifications which it presents are described by
similar terms. Thus we have *simple* and *compound*
fruits; *apocarpous* and *syncarpous* fruits; *superior* and
inferior ones. We speak also of *one-celled, two-celled,*
&c., fruits; and similar kinds of placentation occur in
the fruit as in the ovary.

Composition of the Fruit.—The fruit when perfectly
formed consists of two parts, namely, of a shell or
pericarp, and the seed or seeds contained within it.
The pericarp consists of three layers or regions—an
outer layer or *epicarp;* a middle, the *mesocarp;* and
an inner, the *endocarp.* The middle layer being frequently of a fleshy or succulent nature is also termed
the *sarcocarp;* while the inner layer, from its hardness in some fruits, is likewise called the *stone* or
putamen.

In many fruits these layers are not clearly distinguishable, but in others they may be readily noticed.
Thus in such fruits as the Cherry, Plum, and Peach
the separable skin is the epicarp; the pulpy part, which
is eaten, the mesocarp or sarcocarp; and the stone
enclosing the seed is the endocarp or putamen. In the
Apple and Pear the skin is the epicarp; the fleshy part,
which is eaten, the mesocarp; and the core the endocarp. In the Walnut, the woody shell enveloping the
seed is the endocarp, and the green husk which covers
this consists of the combined mesocarp and epicarp.
In the Orange the outer separable rind is composed of
mesocarp and epicarp; and the thin membranous
partitions which divide the pulp into separate portions
form the endocarp. These examples of fruits, together
with those previously alluded to, will show in a striking

manner the very varying nature and origin of the parts which are commonly eaten.

Dehiscence of the Fruit.—At varying periods, but commonly when the fruit is ripe, the pericarp either opens so as to allow the seeds to escape ; or it remains closed, and the seeds can then only become free by its decay. In the former case the fruit is said to be *dehiscent*, in the latter *indehiscent*. Fruits with hard or fleshy pericarps, such as the Nut, Cherry, Apricot, Apple, Gooseberry, and Orange, are usually indehiscent.

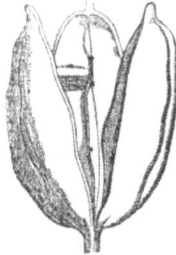 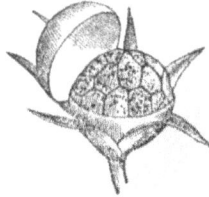

Fig. 95. Fig. 96.

Fig. 95.—Valvular dehiscence of the fruit of the Iris. Fig. 96.—Transverse dehiscence of the fruit of Pimpernel.

Dehiscence may be either partial or complete ; in the latter case the parts into which the fruit separates, which are longitudinally arranged, are termed *valves*, and the fruit is described as *one-valved, two-valved, three-valved* (fig. 95), &c., according to their number.

In other cases dehiscence takes place in a transverse direction, by which the upper part of the fruit separates from the lower, like the lid from a jar or box (fig. 96), when it is called *transverse* ; or it may take place in an irregular manner by little pores or slits, when it is described as *porous*. These pores may be placed either at the apex, sides, or base of the fruits.

Kinds of Fruit.—A great number of fruits have been distinguished by special names, and several classifications have been prepared by botanists ; but in this little book we shall only refer to a few of the more important kinds of fruits.

1. *Fruits formed by a Single Flower:—*
 a. Simple Fruits.
 b. Compound Fruits.
2. *Fruits formed by the combination of several Flowers.*

1. FRUITS FORMED BY A SINGLE FLOWER.

a. SIMPLE FRUITS.—*By a simple fruit we mean one which is formed of but one carpel.*

1. *Legume or Pod.*—This is a superior one-celled fruit, containing one or more seeds, which splits open down the back and front, as in the common Pea, and is hence two-valved (fig. 97).

Fig. 97.   Fig. 98.

2. *Follicle.*—This is a superior one-celled fruit, containing one or more seeds, which opens only down its front, and is hence one-valved (fig. 98).

Fig. 97.—Legume of Pea: *c*, calyx; *ep*, epicarp; *pl*, placenta; *ov*, seeds, attached to the placenta by a stalk, *f*; *en*, endocarp.
Fig. 98.—Follicle of the Columbine.

3. *Drupe or Stone - Fruit.*—Is a superior, one-celled, one or two-seeded, indehiscent fruit, having a fleshy or pulpy sarcocarp, and a hard or stony endocarp, as in the Cherry and Peach, and the pericarp altogether separable into its component parts, namely, of epicarp, sarcocarp, and endocarp.

4. *Achenium or Achene.*—This is a superior, one-celled, one-seeded fruit, with a dry indehiscent pericarp.. Such fruits are frequently mistaken for seeds, but may commonly be distinguished by the remains of the style upon their surface.

b. COMPOUND FRUITS.—*By a compound fruit we mean one which is formed by the more or less complete combination of two or more carpels.*

1. *Capsule.*—This is a superior, one or more celled, many-seeded fruit, with a dry dehiscent pericarp (figs. 95 and 96). Dehiscence may either be valvular, transverse, or porous. It is a very common kind of fruit. A capsule with transverse dehiscence (fig. 96) is frequently called a *pyxis.*

Fig. 99.

2. *Siliqua or Silique.*—This is a superior, long, narrow, many-seeded fruit, divided commonly into two cells by a vertical frame or partition, from which two valves separate from below upwards when ripe, as in the Wallflower and Bitter Cress (fig. 99); when this kind of fruit is short and broad, and contains

Fig. 100.

Fig. 100.—Silicle of Shepherd's Purse.

Fig. 99.—Plant of Hairy Bittercress, showing the Siliques, *f, f,* dehiscing.

but few seeds, it is commonly distinguished as a *Silicula* or *Silicle* (fig. 100).

3. *Berry.*—This is an inferior, one or more celled, many-seeded pulpy fruit. This fruit does not open, and its seeds, which are first firmly attached, ultimately lie loose in the pulp. Examples occur in the Gooseberry and Currant.

A modification of this kind of fruit occurs in the Cucumber and Melon ; the essential difference being that in this fruit, which is called a *pepo*, the seeds which are imbedded in pulp, never become loose, as in the berry.

4. *Pome.*—This is an inferior, two or more celled, few-seeded, indehiscent, fleshy fruit, the endocarp of which is papery, cartilaginous, or bony, and surrounded by a fleshy mass consisting of the combined mesocarp and epicarp. Examples may be seen in the Apple, Pear, and Medlar.

2. FRUITS FORMED BY THE COMBINATION OF SEVERAL FLOWERS.

All fruits thus formed are distinguished by the name of *collective fruits*.

Of these it is only necessary to describe the *Cone,* the fruit of the Fir, Larch, &c. This is a more or less lengthened fruit, composed of a number of hardened scales (figs. 68 and 101), each of which bears at its base one or more naked seeds. When such a fruit is more or less rounded in form instead of conical as in the true cone, and the seeds of the scales much enlarged, as seen in the Cypress, it is then generally termed a *galbulus.*

The fruits of the Hop, Pineapple, Mulberry, and Fig, are also formed by the combination of several flowers, and have received distinctive names, but we cannot refer to them here.

Fig. 101.

Fig. 101.—Cone of Larch.

QUESTIONS.

Of what does the fruit essentially consist ?

2. Explain the term apiculate, and show how small fruits may be distinguished from seeds.

3. What is the nature of the fruit in the Apple and the Strawberry ?

4. What is the composition of the fruit in the Acorn, Filbert, Pineapple, and Fig ?

5. What is meant by the term fruit as botanically applied ?

6. What do we understand by simple and compound, apocarpous and syncarpous, and superior and inferior fruits ?

7. Explain the meaning of pericarp, epicarp, mesocarp, endocarp, sarcocarp, and putamen.

8. Indicate the layers of the pericarp in the Cherry, Plum, and Peach.

9. Describe the pericarp in the Apple, Pear, and Walnut.

10. Indicate the layers of the pericarp in the Orange.

11. Explain the meaning of the term dehiscence as applied to the fruit.

12. What are dehiscent and indehiscent fruits ? Give examples of the latter.

13. What are the valves of the fruit ?

14. Explain the terms valvular, transverse, and porous dehiscence.

KINDS OF FRUIT.

15. What is the simplest arrangement of fruits ?

16. What is meant by a simple fruit ?

17. What is a legume ? Give an example.

18. What is a follicle ?

19. What is a drupe ?

20. What is an achenium ?

21. What is meant by a compound fruit ?

22. What is a capsule ?

23. What is a pyxis ?

24. Define the siliqua and silicula.

25. What is a berry ? Give examples.

26. What is a pepo ? Give examples.

27. What is a pome ? Give examples.

28. What are collective fruits ?

29. What is a cone ? Give examples.

30. What is a galbulus ? Give an example.

31. To what class of fruits do the Hop, Pine-apple, Mulberry and Fig belong ?

---

2. THE SEED.

We have already stated that the ovary contains in its interior one or more little bodies, called *ovules*, which by impregnation become seeds ; but in some plants (as in the Fir and others of the Cone order, and a few other allied orders) the ovules, instead of being enclosed in an ovary, are placed on the margins of altered leaves, or at the base of hardened bracts. Such ovules are therefore called *naked*, and as the seeds of such plants are also necessarily naked they are called *Gymnospermous*, that is, plants with naked seeds; whilst ordinary plants, or those in which the ovules and seeds are distinctly enclosed in an ovary, are termed *Angiospermous*.

The seed is defined as the impregnated ovule, and like it it is either sessile on the placenta, or stalked (fig. 97, *f*), its point of attachment being termed the *hilum*. The number of seeds in the fruit is subject to much variation, and corresponding terms are accordingly employed, as *one-seeded, two-seeded*, &c. The seed may be also either *erect, pendulous*, &c. In form, again, the seed varies much, and is described accordingly as rounded, oval, ovate, &c.

STRUCTURE OF THE SEED.—As already noticed, the seed is essentially composed of two parts, as seen in the Almond (see page 10 and fig. 1), namely, of a *nucleus* or *kernel*, and *integuments*.

1. *Integuments.*—There are commonly two seed-roots or integuments, an outer and an inner. The latter needs no notice here; but the former, which is commonly termed the *testa*, varies in colour, texture, and condition of surface in different seeds, and thus frequently affords important characters by which they can be distinguished from one another. Thus in colour, seeds may be white, black, mottled, &c.; in texture, soft, fleshy, woody, &c.; or present a smooth, wrinkled, or spiny, &c., surface.

Some seeds, again, have winged appendages, and are hence termed *winged;* or when they have a tuft of hairs arising from a particular point, such a tuft is called a *coma*, and the seed is *comose*.

On the surface of some seeds we find small irregular protuberances, which are called *caruncules;* and in other seeds we have an additional integument, to which the name of *aril* has been given. This is generally of a partial nature, and is well seen in the Nutmeg, where it forms the covering, which is commonly known when separated as Mace.

2. *Nucleus or Kernel.*—We have already mentioned that the nucleus of the seed may either consist of the embryo alone (fig. 1), which is alone essential to it, or of the embryo enclosed to a greater or less degree by nourishing matter called the *albumen* (fig. 2, *a*). The structure of the embryo has been already sufficiently described; and with regard to the albumen, it is only necessary for us to say a few words.

Seeds with albumen are called *albuminous*, while those in which it is absent are *exalbuminous*. The albumen varies in amount in different albuminous seeds, and in all cases will be necessarily in inverse proportion to the size of the embryo. The albumen will also vary much in character in different seeds. Thus, in the Wheat and other cereal grains it is filled with starch, and is described accordingly as *mealy* or *farinaceous ;* it is *fleshy* in some seeds ; *oily* in others ; hard and *horny*, as in the Vegetable Ivory Palm, where it constitutes the substance commonly known as vegetable ivory ; and in some few seeds it presents a mottled appearance, as in the Nutmeg and Betel-nut, when it is described as *ruminated*.

QUESTIONS.
1. What are seeds ?
2. What are naked ovules ?
3. What is meant by gymnospermous and angiospermous plants ?
4. What is the hilum of the seed ?
5. Of what is a seed essentially composed ?
6. How many integuments are there in a seed ?
7. What is the testa, and in what ways does it vary ?
8. Explain the terms winged and comose.
9. What is a caruncule ?
10. What is an aril ? Give an example.
11. Of what does the nucleus or kernel of the seed consist ?
12. What is meant by albuminous and exalbuminous seeds ?
13. What is meant by mealy or farinaceous, fleshy, and oily albumen ?
14. What is horny albumen ? Give an example.
15. What is ruminated albumen ? Give examples.

CHAPTER IV.

FLOWERLESS OR CRYPTOGAMOUS PLANTS.

Up to the present our attention has been almost exclusively directed to Flowering Plants, or as they are technically called Phanerogamous Plants; but our sketch of the organs of plants will be incomplete without a brief notice of the other great sub-kingdom of plants called Flowerless or Cryptogamous. The simplest plants of this kind may be seen in the Red Snow, each of which consists simply of a roundish membranous bag or bladder (fig. 102), which is called a *cell*. In other simple plants the cell of which they are constructed is either lengthened so as to assume a tubular form, or branched in various ways; but in all these simple plants we can detect no separation of the nutritive and reproductive functions—

Fig. 102.

Fig. 102.—Several Red Snow plants (magnified).

which is so evident in the higher plants; but the cell of which they are composed is capable of performing both these functions. The plants immediately above these consist of a varying number of cells, either combined in a single row, or variously branched (fig. 103). In these plants we also frequently find one or more of the cells of which they are composed acquiring especial development and producing in their interior a number of others of a smaller size (fig. 103). Here we have the first trace of a separation

Fig. 103.

Fig. 103.—A species of Mould, with two stalks, each terminated by a sac, from which a number of minute spores are escaping.

or distinction of the cells of a plant into those adapted for *nutrition* and those for *reproduction*, as the smaller cells thus developed in the interior of the larger ones are especially designed for reproducing the plant, in the same way as the seeds of Flowering Plants are adapted for that purpose. These reproductive cells are called *spores* (fig. 103).

Fig. 104.

Fig. 104.—Oak Lichen.

In the plants above these simplest ones we find the cells of which they are composed combined in various ways, so as to form flattened leaf-like expansions (figs. 104 and 105) or solid axes (fig. 106), as also special organs of reproduction; but up to this point we have no examples of plants presenting any distinct axis bearing leaves. Such plants are therefore called *Thallophytes* or *Thallogens*; that is, plants consisting of a *thallus*, because the latter term is applied to any filamentous or flattened leaf-expansions, of whatever form, which have no axis or stem distinct from a leaf, but the two combined, as it were, together, and performing the office of both. Under the head of Thallogens we comprise those simpler forms of plants which are commonly known as Sea-weeds, Mushrooms, and Lichens. Again, as

Thallogens are entirely composed of short cells, without any trace of elongated tubular bodies, called wood-cells and vessels (see page 109 and figs. 121 —127), which, with rare exceptions, are found in combination with such cells in all other plants, they are termed *Cellular Plants*, the more highly developed plants placed above them being called *Vascular Plants*.

Fig. 105.

Fig. 105.—Thallus of a Sea Weed.

From Thallogens, by various intermediate stages, we arrive at another order of plants — the true Mosses (fig. 107), which present us with *an evident stem bearing leaves*. In these, also, we find the first trace of roots in the form of little tubular prolongations from the lower part of the stem. In the Mosses, therefore, we have first distinctly shadowed forth the three essential organs of the higher plants, namely, the *root, stem,* and *leaf*. All plants, from the Mosses upwards, are presented to us under ordinary circumstances with a distinct axis, commonly bearing leaves. Such are therefore frequently known as *Cormophytes* or *Cormogens*, signifying stem-producing plants, to distinguish them from the *Thallophytes* or *Thallogens*, just described.

The lowest orders of these stem-producing plants, such as the Mosses (fig. 107), are comparatively insignificant in appearance; and this is even generally the case with Ferns, so far as they are natives of cold and temperate regions, but in

Fig. 106.—Mushrooms.

the warmer parts of the world and in the tropics, the latter plants frequently grow to a considerable height

Fig. 107.—Species of Moss (*Bryum*). Fig. 108.—Spore-case of a Moss: *sp*, sporangium, supported on a stalk, *s*; *per*, peristome; *o*, operculum; *c*, calyptra.

G

and form handsome trees.   These plants, however,
like all previously noticed, are reproduced by *spores*,
and never produce evident flowers like the higher
kind of plants, hence all spore-forming plants are

Fig. 109.   Fig. 110.

Fig. 109.—The Adder's-tongue,
showing the sacs containing the
spores arranged on spike-like processes.   Fig. 110.—Portion of a
frond of the male Fern, with two
sori, *s, s,* covered by an indusium.

denominated   *Flowerless*,   or technically   *Cryptogamous*, that is to say, plants with concealed or invisi-
ble reproductive organs.   Again, as a spore has no
embryo it can have no cotyledon, consequently flowerless plants have been also called *acotyledonous*.   These
Cryptogamous plants are again divided into two groups
called, respectively, *Acrogens* and *Thallogens*, the latter

comprising the simpler forms of plants, which, as previously noticed, are commonly known as Sea-weeds, Mushrooms, and Lichens, and which present no distinction of leaf and stem ; and the former group, such plants as the Mosses and Ferns, which present us with an evident stem bearing leaves.

All plants above the Ferns, from possessing evident flowers or reproductive organs, are termed, as already noticed, Flowering or Phanerogamous plants, and have been fully described in the preceding pages ; and with a brief description of the reproductive organs of Ferns and Mosses we shall conclude this part of our little work.

Fig. 111.

Fig. 111.—Coiled up young fronds of a Fern.

Reproductive Organs of Ferns.—In Ferns the spores or bodies representing the seeds of Flowering plants are contained in little sacs, which are either arranged in clusters on the under surface of the leaves (fig. 110), or on spike-like processes (fig. 109) at their extremities. The leaves, which thus bear the *fructification*, as it is called, are commonly termed *fronds;* and when young are characterised by being coiled up in a circinate manner, like a crosier (fig. 111), in a similar manner to the young flowers in a scorpioid cyme (see page 66). These clusters, which are brown when ripe, are termed *sori.* These sori are either naked, or covered at first by a pale coloured membrane, which is called the *indusium* (fig. 110, *s*). This indusium becomes ultimately wholly or partially detached, and the

Fig. 112.

minute sacs, called *spore-cases* or *sporangia,* of which each sorus is composed, are then exposed to view. If these spore-cases be examined by a magnifying lens, they will be usually found to be stalked and surrounded more or less completely by a ring or *annulus* (fig. 112, *s*); this ring is frequently elastic, and thus causes the bursting of the spore-cases when ripe, so as to allow of the escape of the very minute spores which have been produced within them.

Fig. 112.—*s*, Spore case of a Fern, supported on a stalk, *p*, and surrounded by a ring or annulus.

These spores, which are microscopic cells, are usually somewhat irregular in form, and have two coats. In germination, the inner coat is protruded and ultimately forms a thin green flat leafy expansion, called a *prothallium*, from the under surface of which one or more delicate root-fibres are commonly produced in its earliest stage. On the same under surface we have also developed minute cellular bodies of two distinct kinds, which represent the stamens and carpels of flowering plants. One of these, called an *antheridium* (fig. 113), contains a number of very minute cells, in each of which is a little spirally-waved filament, termed a *spermatozoid*, which performs the same function as the pollen of flowering plants. The other cellular body, representing the carpel of flowering plants, is called an *archegonium ;* it has a little canal in its centre leading to a cavity called the *embryo-sac,* in which is a little cell (*germ-cell*) which is fertilised by the contact of the spermatozoids of the antheridia, and the result is the formation of a new plant, resembling the one from which the spore was originally derived.

Fig. 113.

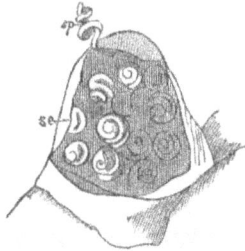

Fig. 113.—Side view of an antheridium of a Fern, containing a number of sperm-cells, *se; sp,* spermatozoids escaping after having burst the sperm-cells.

The difference between the germination of a spore of a Fern and that of a seed is thus seen to consist in the fact that a seed directly produces a new plant in the process of germination; but a spore forms in the first case a thalloid expansion on which the bodies are produced, which by their mutual action cause the development of a new plant. This has been called an *alternation of generations.*

Reproductive Organs of Mosses.—In Mosses the *sporangia* or spore-cases are placed upon hair-like stalks or setæ. Each of these spore-cases, when fully formed, is a hollow urn-like case (fig. 108, *sp*), which is covered at first by a kind of hood or *calyptra, c.* When this is removed the sporange is observed to be closed by a lid or *operculum, o ;* and when this is separated the mouth of the spore-case is seen with its margin commonly surrounded by one or two rows of teeth, forming collectively what has been termed the *peristome, per.* These teeth are either four in number, or some multiple of four.

In *germination* the spores which are contained within these spore-cases at first produce a plant with rootlets, branches, and leaves, upon the leafy shoots of which antheridia and archegonia are developed, as on the prothallium of Ferns, the result of the mutual action of which is the formation of the sporangia containing spores, as just described.

Besides the Ferns and Mosses now described, all Cryptogamous plants have reproductive organs which perform analogous purposes to the stamens and carpels of flowering plants, hence such plants are not *asexual*, as was formerly supposed, but only *Cryptogamous*, that is, literally, with the sexes concealed or obscure.

The further description of the reproductive organs of Flowerless Plants would be out of place in this little work.

QUESTIONS.

1. What is the structure of the simplest flowerless plants?
2. What is the structure of the flowerless plants immediately above such, as the Red Snow, and what provision is made in them for reproduction?
3 What are the reproductive bodies of the flowerless plants called?
4. What is a thallus, and what are Thallogens?
5. What plants are included in the Thallogens?
6. What are cellular plants?
7. What are vascular plants?
8. Give a general description of a Moss.
9. What are Cormogens?
10. Why are flowerless plants also called cryptogamous?
11. Why are such plants called acotyledonous?
12. What are acrogens, and what plants are included in them?
13. What are all plants above the Ferns called?
14. What are fronds?
15. Describe the fructification of a Fern.
16. What is a prothallium, and how is it formed?
17. What is an antheridium, and what is its structure?
18. What is an archegonium, and what is its structure?
19. What is meant by alternation of generations?
20. Describe the fructification of a Moss.
21. How do the spores of mosses germinate?
22. Is the term asexual properly applied to flowerless plants?

PART II.

We have hitherto only given a general sketch of the various organs of a plant as they are presented to us on the most superficial examination by the naked eye. But if these several organs be more minutely examined by the aid of the microscope, it will be found that they are made up of others of a simpler kind in the form of little membranous closed sacs, called cells, and elongated tubular bodies of various forms, sizes, and appearances. Hence, in describing a plant with reference to its structure, we have two classes of organs to allude to, namely, the compound organs or those which are visible to the naked eye—as the root, stem, leaf, and the parts of the flower; and the elementary structures of which these compound organs are composed. A comprehensive knowledge of these elementary structures, or building materials of plants, is of course essential to a complete and satisfactory acquaintance with the compound organs; but it will only be necessary for our purpose to give a very brief sketch of the subject. The description of this elementary structure of plants is termed *Vegetable Histology.*

CHAPTER I.

VEGETABLE HISTOLOGY; OR ELEMENTARY STRUCTURE OF PLANTS.

SECTION I.—OF THE CELL AS AN INDIVIDUAL.

All plants in their earliest condition are composed of one or more delicate membranous closed sacs, called *cells.* All the organs which are afterwards found in the plant are also made up of various modifications of these structures. The cell is therefore the first and only elementary organ of a plant, namely, that from which all the other organs, however complicated, are derived. It will be necessary, therefore, for us to describe this cell as fully as we are able.

1. FORM AND SIZE OF CELLS.—*a. Form.*—In its earliest condition, the cell consists of an exceedingly thin structureless membrane, enclosing various substances; and when developed in a space where it is perfectly free from pressure, and when equally nourished at all parts of its surface, it assumes a more or less rounded form (fig. 102). But in consequence of cells being usually developed in a more or less confined space, where they are subjected to varying pressure from the surrounding organs, and unequally nourished at their different parts, they assume a number of other forms, as *elliptic, angular, fusiform, cylindrical,* &c. (figs. 115 to 121).

The description of all these varying forms of cells is unnecessary; it will be sufficient for us to say that all cells, so far as their forms are concerned, may be divided into the *short* and *long*. The *short cells* when combined together so as to form a tissue, are bounded by plane or rounded surfaces (figs. 115 and 120), so that they simply touch each other at their sides or by their flattened ends; but the *long cells,* having commonly tapering extremities, when they combine together, overlap one another, and become interposed between the sides of the cells which are placed above and below them (figs. 116 and 121). Another distinction commonly observed also between the short and long cells, consists in their cell-walls; thus the walls of the short cells are usually thin, while those of the lengthened cells are more or less thickened by the deposition of incrusting matters upon their inner surfaces (fig. 121).

From this description of the short and long cells, it will be seen that the latter are admirably adapted for those parts of a plant where strength and firmness are required, and that the former are only suited for soft structures.

b. Size.—Whether cells are short or long, they are essentially microscopic, for it is only in very rare cases, as in certain water plants, that they are sufficiently large as to be visible by the naked eye. In the short cells the two diameters do not present any striking differences as to size, and these commonly vary from about $\frac{1}{250}$ to $\frac{1}{1200}$ of an inch; but in the lengthened cells, while their transverse diameter is frequently less than the $\frac{1}{1500}$ of an inch, they are sometimes a quarter of an inch or more in length.

2. CELL-WALL OR CELL-MEMBRANE, AND CONTENTS OF CELLS.—*a. Cell-Wall.*—The membrane which constitutes the walls of cells is at first very thin, transparent, and colourless, and readily permeable to fluids; but as it increases in age, it frequently becomes coloured, and is thickened by the successive deposit of new matter upon its inner surface (fig. 114). These thickening layers are commonly called *secondary layers* or *deposits;* and it is to them that the hardness and firmness of wood and the stones of fruits are due. From their common occurrence in wood, the **term** *lignin* is also frequently applied to these deposits.

When the membrane is first deposited it is seen, when examined by a microscope, to be perfectly homogeneous in appearance like a piece of the clearest glass; but when thickened by

Fig. 114.

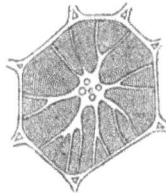

Fig. 114.—Transverse section of a thickened cell-wall, showing secondary layers.

secondary layers, as these are not imperforate like the membrane constituting the original cell-wall, but either perforated so as to resemble a sieve, or forming delicate threads or bands arranged in a more or less spiral direction on its inner surface, the membrane then presents, when viewed by transmitted light under the microscope, numerous transparent slits or dots (fig. 115), or dots surrounded by discs (fig. 116), or a more or less spiral character (fig. 117); and we have thus formed various kinds of Pitted and Spiral Cells.

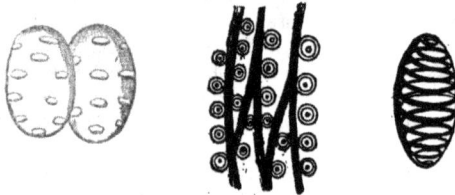

Fig. 115.—Pitted Cells. Fig. 116.—Disc-bearing wood-cells of the Fir. Fig. 117.—Spiral Cell.

b. Contents of Cells.—When young, cells are filled with a viscid nearly colourless fluid, called *protoplasm*, in which may be seen one or more little bodies, called *Nuclei* (fig. 118), in which are placed one or more bright spots, called *Nucleoli*. The presence of this fluid with its Nuclei is evidence that the cells are in an active vital state, and hence in all the growing parts of plants such cells are found. But as the cells increase in age, this viscid fluid gradually becomes replaced by a watery fluid called the *sap*, in which a great variety of other substances are either dissolved or found floating. The more important of these are *chlorophyll, starch,* and *raphides*.

Chlorophyll is the name applied to the green colouring matter of plants. It generally occurs in the form of granules, which float in the sap, and is only formed under the influence of light, and therefore is found only on the parts of plants near their surface. It is for this reason that when plants grow in the dark they present a blanched appearance.

The peculiar tints of the petals, and of other parts not green, are also due to colouring matters of various kinds, which are contained in the cells of which such parts are made up. These colouring matters are frequently comprised under the common name of *chromule*.

Fig. 118.   Fig. 119.   Fig. 120.

Fig. 118.—Cell with nucleus and nucleolus. Fig. 119.—Cell of the Potato containing starch-granules. Fig. 120.—Three cells of the Common Beet, one of which contains crystals or raphides.

Starch also occurs commonly in the form of granules, which vary in form, size, and appearance in different plants (fig. 119). Arrowroot, sago, and potato starch may be mentioned as familiar examples of starches. It commonly occurs only in the internal and subterranean parts of a plant, or those removed from light, in which respects it presents a marked contrast to chlorophyll. Starch is among the most abundant and most universally distributed of all the cell-contents of plants.

Raphides.—This term, which is the Greek for needles, was originally only given to those crystals of plants which were shaped like a needle, but the name is now applied to crystals of any form found in the cells of plants (fig. 120). In some plants these crystals are so abundant that their dried parts are perceptibly gritty when chewed, as for instance rhubarb root.

QUESTIONS.

1. What is the microscopic structure of plants?
2. What is meant by compound organs, and what by elementary structures?
3. What is meant by vegetable histology?
4. What is a cell?
5. What is the typical form of a cell, and how are other forms produced?

6. Describe the general characters of the short and long cells.
7. In what parts of a plant are short and long cells found?
8. What is the size of the short cells?
9. What is the size of the long cells?
10. What are the characters of the cell-wall of young cells, and how is it thickened?
11. What are the thickening layers called?
12. What differences are produced in the appearance of the cell-wall by the deposition of secondary layers?
13. What are pitted and spiral cells?
14. What is protoplasm, and what is its presence in the cell evidence of?
15. What are nuclei and nucleoli?
16. What is the sap of plants?
17. What is chlorophyll, and where is it found?
18. What is chromule?
19. In what form, and in what parts of plants is starch found?
20. What are raphides?
21. Are raphides abundant in any plants?

SECTION II.—CELLS IN COMBINATION.

We have already mentioned that cells, so far as their forms are concerned, may be divided into the short and long. But besides these long cells we have other tubular organs in plants which are termed *vessels*. These latter organs are either formed directly from lengthened cells, or, as is far more generally the case, from a row of cylindrical cells placed end to end, the intervening partitions of which have been absorbed, so that their cavities form a continuous canal. By the combination together of the short and long cells and vessels we have compound structures formed, which are called Tissues.

1. CELLULAR TISSUE.—This is composed of commonly thin-walled cells, whose length does not much exceed their breadth, or in which the proportion of the two diameters does not vary to any great extent. This tissue, as already noticed, constitutes the entire structure of the lower order of plants or Thallogens, which are hence frequently termed Cellular plants; and it forms all the soft parts of Vascular plants (see page 96) ; and in cultivating plants or parts of plants

for culinary purposes and for food generally, the great object aimed at is to develop this kind of tissue as far as possible.

2. Woody Tissue.—This is composed of very long thick-walled cells with tapering extremities (fig. 121), which when in contact overlap each other so as to form a very compact and firm tissue. The woody portions of all plants consist in a great degree of this form of tissue, as well as the inner bark of trees and the veins of leaves—in fact all parts where great firmness and toughness are required.

From the characters of this tissue it is admirably adapted for various textile fabrics and for paper-making. Hemp, flax, jute, and china-grass are familiar examples of such tissues (or, as they are commonly called, *fibres*), which are in use for such purposes.

Fig. 121.

Fig. 121. — Wood-cells with thickened walls.

Fig. 122.   Fig. 123.   Fig. 124.   Fig. 125.   Fig. 126.

Fig. 122.—Pitted vessel.   Fig. 123.—Spiral vessels.   Fig. 124.—Annular vessel.   Fig. 125.—Reticulated vessel.   Fig. 126.—Scalariform vessels.

3. VASCULAR TISSUE.—This tissue is commonly associated with woody tissue, so as to constitute the hard parts of plants. It is composed of elongated tubular organs, but larger than the elongated cells of which woody tissue is formed. There are several varieties of vessels, the nature of which essentially depends upon the different kinds of cells out of which they have been constructed. Thus we have *pitted vessels*, the largest of all which occur in plants, which present a pitted or dotted appearance (fig. 122); *spiral vessels*, which have their inside occupied by one or more elastic spirally-coiled fibres running from one end to the other (fig. 123); *annular, reticulated,* and *scalariform* or *ladder-like vessels* (figs. 124 to 126), which are marked on their inside by fibres arranged in rings, reticulations, or in bars over one

Fig. 127.

another, like the steps of a ladder; or, lastly, *laticiferous vessels*, which are long branched tubes (fig. 127) uniting freely with each other like the veins of animals, and containing the milky juice of plants, which is called *latex*.

By the combination together of the various kinds of cells and vessels now described the main fabric of the plant is made up. The lower plants of Thallogens are composed entirely of Cellular Tissue; but all plants above them consist partly of Cellular Tissue and partly of a tissue formed by the combination of Woody Tissue and vessels of different kinds, and which is therefore commonly known under the name of *Fibrovascular Tissue*.

Fig. 127.—
Laticiferous vessels.

4. EPIDERMAL TISSUE.—In all the higher Flowerless, and generally in Flowering plants, the surface of the different organs is invested by a layer (fig. 128), which is formed of flattened cells called *tabular*, and covered by a thin transparent pellicle. This investing layer is

called the *general integument*, or, technically, *Epidermal Tissue*. The inner cellular portion, *e, e*, is called the *epidermis*; and the outer pellicle, *p, p*, the *cuticle*.

Fig. 128.

The epidermis covers all the parts of plants upon which it is found that are directly exposed to the air, except the stigma of flowering plants; and it is in all cases absent from those which live under water. In such parts, and also in Thallogens, which have no true epidermis, the surface is invested by cuticle only.

Fig. 128.—Epidermal tissue from the leaf of an Iris: *p, p*, cuticle; *s, s*, stomates; *e, e*, epidermal cells.

Stomates.—Between some of the epidermal cells, and opening into the intercellular cavities beneath them, are certain orifices which, from having some faint resemblance to the lips and mouth of an animal, are called stomates, from a Greek word signifying a mouth (fig. 128, *s, s*). These orifices, which vary very much in number, form, and arrangement in different plants, and which are commonly most abundant on the under surface of leaves, are especially designed to allow a free communication between the internal tissues of the plant and the atmosphere.

Hairs and Glands.—These have been already noticed in speaking of leaves (see page 40). They consist of one or more cells, variously combined, and with varying contents, which are directly connected with the surface of plants—that is, the epidermis, and hence they are commonly known as *appendages of the epidermis.* We have already seen that they vary much in form, appearance, and nature, and, so far as their more important modifications, have been already sufficiently described.

5. INTERCELLULAR SYSTEM.—As the different kinds of cells are very frequently bounded by rounded surfaces,

or more or less irregular outlines, it must necessarily happen that when they come in contact they can only touch each other at certain points, by which interspaces will be left between them, the size of which will vary according to the greater or less roundness or irregularity of their surfaces; these constitute the *intercellular system*. In some cases these interspaces are filled up with solid matter, which glues, as it were, the cells together; this matter is called *intercellular substance*, and is analogous in its nature to the cuticle already described. In other cases these interspaces form continuous canals, called *intercellular canals* or *passages;* or large circumscribed cavities called *intercellular spaces*. These spaces are either filled with air, and are then termed *air cavities*, or with the peculiar secretions of the plant, when they are distinguished under the name of *receptacles of secretion*.

QUESTIONS.

1. What are the vessels of plants?
2. What is meant by cellular tissue?
3. In what plants and parts of plants do we find cellular tissue?
4. What is woody tissue?
5. Where is woody tissue found?
6. For what purposes is woody tissue especially adapted?
7. What is vascular tissue?
8. What are pitted vessels?
9. What are spiral vessels?
10. What are annular, reticulated, and scalariform vessels?
11. What are laticiferous vessels?
12. What is the structure of Thallogens?
13. Of what tissues are plants made up which are above the Thallogens?
14. What is epidermal tissue, where is it found, and of what does it consist?
15. What is the epidermis, and where is it found?
16. In what plants does the cuticle replace the epidermis?
17. What are stomates?
18. What are hairs and glands?
19. What is meant by appendages of the epidermis?
20. What is meant by the intercellular system?
21. What is intercellular substance?
22. What are intercellular canals, intercellular passages, and intercellular spaces?
23. What are air cavities?
24. What do you understand by a receptacle of secretion?

CHAPTER II.

ORGANS OF NUTRITION.

SECTION I.—OF THE STEM OR ASCENDING AXIS.

In the first part of this little work we commenced our description of the organs of nutrition with the root, but so far as internal structure is concerned it is far better to treat of the stem first, and afterwards, when noticing the root, allude especially to those characters by which it is distinguished from the stem. A stem in its simplest condition, as in Mosses (fig. 107), consists merely of ordinary cellular tissue, strengthened by a central bundle of woody tissue; but in all plants above the Mosses the stem is made up partly of cellular tissue and partly of fibro-vascular, and hence in describing the internal structure of such stems we have to distinguish the *cellular system*, which forms their soft portions, and the *fibro-vascular system*, which constitutes their hard parts, and gives them their requisite strength and toughness.

In their internal structure the stems of plants are subject to numerous modifications, all of which are in a great measure due to the different ways in which the fibro-vascular system is distributed amidst the cellular. All these modifications may be, however, in their essential characters reduced to three, two of which are found in Flowering, and one in Flowerless plants. As illustrations of the two former, we will take an Oak and a Palm stem; and of the latter, the stem of a Tree-fern.

Upon making a transverse section of an Oak stem (fig. 129) we find that the two systems are so arranged as to exhibit a distinct separation of parts. Thus we have a central one, *m*, called the *pith;* an external part, *c, e,* or *bark;* an intermediate portion or *wood, r,* dispersed in concentric layers; and little rays, *b*, connecting the pith and the bark, termed *medullary rays.*

H

Such a stem grows essentially in diameter by successive additions of new matter on the outside of its wood, and hence it is called Exogenous (from two Greek words signifying *outside growers*).

Fig. 129.   Fig. 130.

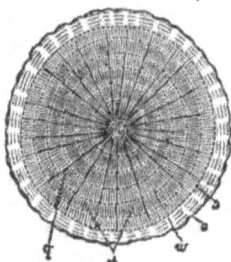 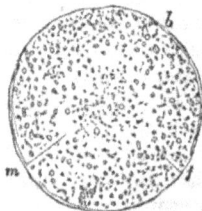

Fig. 129.—Transverse section of an Oak Branch, six years old: *m*, pith; *c, e*, bark; *r*, wood; *b*, medullary rays. Fig. 130.—Transverse section of the stem of a Palm: *m*, cellular substance; *f*, fibrovascular bundles; *b*, rind or false bark.

In a transverse section of a Palm stem (fig. 130) no such separation of parts can be noticed, but upon making a transverse section we observe a general mass of cellular tissue, *m*, and the fibro-vascular system scattered irregularly throughout this in the form of separate bundles, *f*; and the whole is covered externally by a kind of rind or false bark, *b*. Such a stem grows by the addition of new bundles, which are directed at first towards its interior, and hence it is called Endogenous (from two Greek words signifying *inside growers*.)

Upon making a transverse section of a Tree-fern (fig. 131) we observe the centre, *m*, to be either hollow or filled with cellular tissue, the fibro-vascular system being arranged in irregular sinuous or wavy plates around it, *v v*, and forming a continuous or interrupted circle near the circumference, which consists of a rind, *e*, inseparable from the wood beneath. Such a stem only grows by addition to its summit, and is hence called Acrogenous (from two Greek words signifying *summit growers*).

Plants presenting the three kinds of stem just noticed exhibit certain differences in the structure of their embryo. Thus plants with Exogenous stems have an embryo with *two* cotyledons (figs. 1 and 3); those with Endogenous stems have but *one* cotyledon in their embryo (fig. 2), while those with Acrogenous stems have no proper embryo, and consequently *no* cotyledons. Hence exogenous stems are also termed *Dicotyledonous*, endogenous stems *Monocotyledonous*, and acrogenous stems *Acotyledonous*.

Fig. 131.

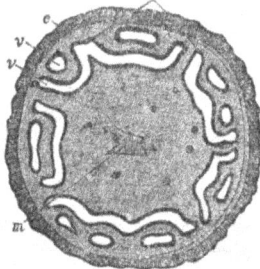

Fig. 131.—Transverse section of the stem of a Tree Fern: *m*, cellular tissue, which is wanting in the centre; *v, v*, fibro-vascular bundles; *e*, rind.

We must now describe briefly these three kinds of stems, commencing with that presenting exogenous structure.

1. EXOGENOUS STEM.—All the trees and large shrubs of this country, and those of temperate and cold climates, are exogenous in their growth. In warm and tropical climates such plants occur associated with those possessing endogenous and acrogenous structure, but exogenous plants are far the most abundant even in these parts of the globe.

An exogenous stem presents, as we have seen, four distinct parts, namely, *pith, wood, medullary rays*, and *bark*. These must be separately described.

1. *Pith* (figs. 129 and 132, *m*).—This is commonly a continuous column of cellular tissue, as may be well seen in the Elder, situated at, or towards, the centre of the stem. It is not continued into the root, but is at first

H 2

always connected with the terminal and lateral leaf-buds. The cells of which it is composed present an angular form (fig. 132, *m*). When first produced it has a greenish colour and is soft and juicy, and is then in an active condition, but after the first year its activity ceases; it no longer increases in thickness, and it soon becomes dry and colourless, and commonly more or less broken up, so as no longer to form a continuous column.

2. *Wood.*—This is placed between the pith and the bark, and is separated into wedge-shaped bundles by the passage through it of the medullary rays.

For each year's growth of the wood we have one circle or zone of wood, the zones of successive years being placed on the outside of the previous ones, and hence the name exogenous which is applied to such stems (fig. 129, *r*). Each of these zones, except that of the first year, has essentially the same structure, and consists of woody tissue (fig. 132, *fl*), among which are distributed, in varying abundance in different plants, some

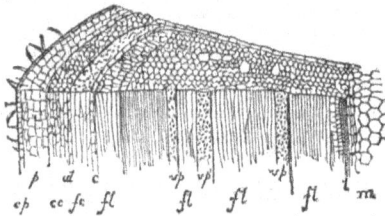

Fig. 132.

Fig. 132.—Vertical section of a young branch of Common Maple magnified : *m*, pith; *t*, spiral vessels ; *fl*, woody tissue ; *vp*, pitted vessels; *c*, cambium layer ; *fc*, liber tissue ; *vl*, laticiferous vessels ; *cc*, middle layer of bark ; *p*, corky layer of bark ; *ep*, epidermis.

vessels which in perennial plants are principally of the kind called pitted, *vp* ; but in herbaceous stems other vessels, such as annular, also occur. The vessels may be readily known in a transverse section by the large size of their openings.

The zone forming the first year's growth has the same structure as the zones of successive years, but with the addition of an interrupted sheath of spiral vessels on its inside immediately surrounding the pith (*medulla*), and to which the name of *medullary sheath* is commonly applied (fig. 132, *t*).

The structure of the zones is also somewhat different in certain plants. Thus in those of the Fir tribe, and in all Gymnospermous plants, there are but few or any pitted vessels, and the cells of which the woody tissue is made up are larger than those of ordinary woody tissue, and have peculiar markings in the form of little circles or discs surrounding a central dot (fig. 116).

These layers of wood are formed in successive zones from a layer of vitally active cells, that is, cells containing protoplasm, &c., which is placed on their outside, and to which the name of *cambium layer* or *cambium* has been given (fig. 132, *c*). From the same cambium new bark is also formed each year; and as the bark is placed outside the wood it is endogenous in its growth, instead of exogenous as the wood.

The annual layers of wood when first formed are in an active condition, their component structures being gorged with fluid or sap, which they are transmitting upwards from the root to the leaves. As they increase in age, however, their walls become thickened by various deposits from the sap, of which they are the carriers, so that their cavities become ultimately nearly obliterated, and are thus rendered almost or quite impervious. This change is more especially evident in such trees as the Ebony, Mahogany, and Lignum Vitæ, where the thickening deposits are of a coloured nature. The value of wood as timber depends chiefly upon the character of this incrusting matter, and is commonly in proportion to its colour; hence coloured woods are far harder and more durable than *white woods*, such as the Poplar and the Willow.

As all the active processes of an exogenous plant are thus carried on in the outer layers of the wood, we have an explanation of the reason why a plant continues to live and put forth new branches when its central part is destroyed, as we find is frequently the case in the trunks of old trees.

The two portions of the wood thus readily distinguishable in most plants receive different names. The soft, new, outer, colourless wood, is termed the *Sap-wood* or *Alburnum;* and the hard, older, dry, coloured wood, is called the *Heart-wood* or *Duramen.*

Age and Size of Trees.—a. Age.—As each zone of wood in an exogenous stem is produced annually, it should follow that by counting the number of zones as seen in a transverse section of the wood of a tree we ought to be able to ascertain its age; and this is true, with a few exceptions, when such trees are natives of cold and temperate climates, because in these we have a winter where there is a cessation of growth, and consequently the limits of each zone are accurately defined. But in such trees, when grown in warm climates, it is generally difficult, and in some cases impossible, to ascertain their age in this manner. This arises either from certain peculiarities of growth, or, far more frequently, because there is no complete season of repose in such regions, and hence the annual zones are often indistinct, and not therefore readily distinguishable from one another.

Exogenous trees frequently live to a great age, and although it is probable that in some cases their age has been overrated, it seems tolerably certain that Yews will live at least 1,500 years, Oaks 1,200, Lime Trees 1,200, and Olives 1,000 years. Other trees, such as the Mammoth Pine of Oregon (*Wellingtonia gigantea*), probably attain to at least 3,000 years old, and when we find that these trees have been seen 450 feet high, such an age would appear to be by no means an extravagant estimate.

b. Size.—Trees not only live to a great age, but they also frequently attain an enormous size, which indeed is in itself, in some degree at least, a proof of their great age. Thus the Mammoth tree just mentioned has been measured 116 feet in circumference at the base; the Chestnut tree of Mount Etna is 180 feet in girth; some

Cedars of Lebanon have a girth of more than 40 feet; and even Oaks in this country have been measured more than 50 feet in circumference.

3. *Medullary Rays.*—These consist of flattened six-sided cells, called tabular cells, which are placed one above the other like the bricks in a wall, and are so arranged that in a transverse section of the wood they are seen as fine lines connecting the pith and the bark (fig. 129, *b*). The medullary rays constitute the *silver-grain* of cabinet-makers, and it is to their presence and characters, more than to any other cause, that the varying appearance of different woods is due.

4. *Bark.*—The bark is situated on the outside of the stem immediately surrounding the wood, to which it is organically connected by the cambium layer and medullary rays (figs. 129, *c*, *e*, and 132). When fully formed it consists of three distinct layers, the two outer of which belong to the cellular system, and the inner to the fibro-vascular. The *outer layer* consists of flattened tabular cells, and has a corky texture, and is hence frequently called the *corky layer* (fig. 132, *p*). It is this layer which in the Cork-oak constitutes the very valuable substance known as Cork; and it is this layer also which gives to the young bark of trees their peculiar colour, that is, other than green. The *middle layer*, *c*, is composed of angular cells filled with chlorophyll, by which it may be distinguished from the outer layer; and it is also from this cause that it is called the *green layer*.

The *inner layer* (fig. 132, *fc* and *vl*) is by far the most important, as it continues in an active state, like the outer zones of the wood, as long as the plant lives, which is not the case with the two outer layers of the bark, which lose their vitality after having arrived at a certain age. This inner bark consists of thick-sided, very tough woody tissue called *liber tissue*, *fc*, bound together by cellular tissue, and containing also some laticiferous vessels, *vl*.

This inner bark is commonly known as the *liber*

because after a few years' growth it may be separated
into thin layers (which represent annual growths) like
the leaves of a book; or this name may have been
derived from this layer of the bark having formerly been
used for writing upon.

2. ENDOGENOUS STEM.—In this country, as already
stated, there are no indigenous trees or large shrubs
exhibiting this mode of growth, although we have
numerous herbaceous plants, such as Grasses, Rushes,
&c., which do so. But it is in warmer regions, and
especially in the tropics, where we find the most
striking and characteristic illustrations of such stems,
and of these the Palms are by far the most remarkable.
The appearance of such plants, even externally, is very
different from that of exogenous trees, for the stems of
Palms are commonly of the same diameter throughout,
being uniformly cylindrical from below upwards, instead
of conical, as is the case with those of exogenous trees,
and frequently rise to the height of 150 feet or more,
usually without branching, but crowned at their summit
by an enormous tuft of leaves.

Upon making a transverse section of a Palm stem
(fig. 130) we find, as already noticed (page 114), no such
separation of parts into pith, wood, medullary rays, and
bark, as occurs in an exogenous stem; but the cellular
system, m, is more or less diffused over the entire
surface of the section, while the fibro-vascular system, f,
is arranged vertically in this in the form of separate
bundles, and the whole is covered externally by a cellular
and fibrous layer called the *false bark* or *rind*, b.

Internal Structure.—In such stems, as in those of
exogenous plants, we have both a cellular and fibro-
vascular system to describe, but we have but few
remarks to make as regards the cellular system. This
commonly consists of angular cells, the walls of which
are soft and thin in herbaceous plants, but thickened
and hard like wood in endogenous trees, such as Palms,
serving thus to bind the separate fibro-vascular bundles
into a hard wood-like mass.

The great peculiarities of an endogenous stem essentially depend upon the *fibro-vascular system*. The separate
vascular bundles, as they are commonly called, of which
this is composed, may be traced to the leaves, from which
organs they are at first directed towards the interior of
the stem, along which they generally descend for some
distance, and then gradually curve outwards again, and
terminate at the circumference (fig. 133). The bundles
consist at first of cellular tissue,
in which are dispersed woody
tissue and vessels of different
kinds, but in their progress
downwards they gradually lose
the vessels, and on their termination at the circumference they
consist simply of woody tissue
bound together by cellular tissue;
and it is the ends of these vascular bundles which form the
false bark of such trees.

As the bundles are successively
developed, they are always deposited at first towards the centre,
that is, within those previously
formed. Hence it naturally follows that the latter will be gradually pushed outwards, so that the
outside of such stems will always
exhibit a closer aggregation of
bundles than the inside, and in
such stems, therefore, the hardest
part is on the outside, and the
softest inside, directly the reverse of what occurs in
those of exogenous growth. From their mode of growth
such stems are therefore called *endogenous*, a term,
however, which is not strictly correct, for although the
bundles are internal above, they are external below.

Age of Endogenous Stems.—There is no such satisfactory means of ascertaining the age of such trees as those

Fig. 133. ,

Fig. 133. — Diagram
showing the course of the
fibro-vascular bundles in
an endogenous stem: *a, b,
c, d,* fibro-vascular bundles, showing their course
down the stem.

of exogenous plants, for there is nothing in their internal
structure which will give us any clue for its determina-
tion. The best means of ascertaining the age of Palms
is by noting their increase in height in any one year's
growth, and then as such stems grow almost uniformly
in length in successive years, by knowing their height
and annual growth we can approximately determine their
age. It is obvious, however, that such a mode of ascertaining the age of endogenous trees is of limited
applicability, and it is moreover by no means to be
depended upon.

8. ACROGENOUS STEM.—The simplest form of such a
stem is seen in Mosses (fig. 107), and the highest in
Ferns (fig. 111). In this country Ferns even are but
insignificant illustrations of acrogenous growth, for in
our Ferns the stem merely runs along the ground, or
burrows more or less beneath it, and sends up its leaves,
or fronds as they are more properly called (page 99),
into the air, which die down yearly. But in warm
regions, and more especially in the tropics, we find
Ferns in the highest state of development. Here the
stem rises to the height of fifty, sixty, or more feet, and
bears at its summit a tuft of leaves. In their external
appearance, therefore, Tree-ferns have great resemblance
to Palms in bearing their foliage at their summit, in
having no lateral buds to produce branches, and from
being of nearly uniform diameter from below upwards.

Internal Structure.—The appearance which a Tree-
fern stem presents upon making a transverse section
has been already described (page 114). The cellular
system, which is only clearly observable in young stems
(the centre being hollow in old trees), is composed of
thin-walled angular cells, and is analogous to the pith
of exogenous plants. The fibro-vascular system forming
the wood is arranged in the form of wavy plates forming
a continuous or interrupted circle just within the circumference (fig. 131). These plates or fibro-vascular bundles
consist externally of thick-sided, dark, hard, woody
tissue, enclosing cellular tissue, in which ladder-like

vessels are more especially to be found. On the outside of the stem we have a hard *rind*, which is composed of hard dark-coloured woody tissue, covered externally by cellular tissue.

Such stems grow by additions to their summit, and hence they are called *acrogenous*; the stem in reality being here formed of the bases of the leaves or fronds which carry up the growing point with them.

There is nothing in the internal structure or external appearance of such stems to indicate their age.

QUESTIONS.

1. What is the structure of the stem of a moss?
2. Of what structures do the stems of all plants above mosses consist?
3. How many principal modifications of stems are found, and in what plants?
4. What are the parts seen in a transverse section of an oak stem?
5. What is meant by the term exogenous?
6. What are the parts seen in a transverse section of a palm stem?
7. What is meant by the term endogenous?
8. What do we observe in a transverse section of a tree-fern?
9. What do we mean by the term acrogenous?
10. In what class of plants are exogenous stems found?
11. In what class of plants are endogenous stems found?
12. In what class of plants are acrogenous stems found?

1. Exogenous Stem.

13. Where are exogenous trees found?
14. What are the parts of an exogenous stem?
15. What is the pith, and with what parts is it connected?
16. What is the structure of the pith, and what is its appearance in young and old stems?
17. Where is the wood situated, and how is it arranged?
18. What is the result of each year's growth of the wood?
19. Of what structures are the annual zones composed?
20. How may the vessels of the wood be known?
21. What is the difference in structure between the zone of the first and successive years?
22. What peculiarities of structure does the wood of gymnospermous plants present?
23. What is the cambium layer, and what parts are developed from it?
24. What are the differences between the zones of wood when first formed and when they have arrived at a certain age?
25. In what plants are such differences most clearly visible?
26. What are white woods?

27. What woods are most valuable as timber?
28. Which is the most active part of the wood?
29. Explain the reason why the centre of the wood may be destroyed, and the plant continue to live.
30. Explain the terms alburnum and duramen.
31. How would you ascertain the age of a tree?
32. Is it possible to ascertain the age of exogenous trees with equal facility in both cold and warm climates?
33. What interferes with the distinctness of the annual layers of exogenous trees in warm climates?
34. Give some examples of the age of trees.
35. What is the height of the Mammoth tree?
36. Give some examples of trees of large size.
37. What are medullary rays?
38. What is the silver grain?
39. Where is the bark placed, and of what does it consist?
40. Describe the structure of the outer layer of the bark.
41. Why is it called the corky layer?
42. What is the structure of the middle layer?
43. Why is it called the green layer?
44. In what respect is the inner layer the most important part of the bark?
45. What is the structure of the inner layer?
46. Why is it called liber?

2. ENDOGENOUS STEM.

47. Where are endogenous trees especially found?
48. In what particulars do Palms in their external appearance differ from exogenous trees?
49. What do we see in a transverse section of a Palm stem?
50. What is the false bark or rind?
51. What is the structure of the cellular system of an endogenous plant?
52. Describe the growth of the vascular bundles.
53. What is the structure of a vascular bundle?
54. Which is the hardest part of the stem of a palm, and the cause which leads to it?
55. What is the origin of the term endogenous?
56. How is the age of an endogenous plant determined?
57. Is the calculated age of endogenous plants to be depended upon?

3. ACROGENOUS STEM.

58. What is the simplest form of an acrogenous stem, and what the highest?
59. In what do ferns of this country differ in their general appearance from those of warmer regions?
60. What is the external appearance of a tree-fern?
61. In what respects does it resemble a palm?
62. What are the appearances presented by a transverse section of a tree-fern?
63. Describe the cellular system of a tree-fern.
64. Describe the fibro-vascular system of a tree-fern.

65. Of what does the rind of a tree-fern consist?
66. How does a tree-fern grow?
67. What is meant by the term acrogenous?
68. Is there any means of ascertaining the age of a tree-fern?

SECTION II.—OF THE ROOT OR DESCENDING AXIS.

In its growth and internal structure the root, in nearly all its essential characters, resembles the stem; but it presents certain peculiarities which we now proceed to describe. In the first place, roots do not grow throughout their entire length like stems, but only just within their extremities, which are gradually pushed forward and renewed. Thus the apex of a root is always clothed by a layer of denser tissue than that which is within it, and this forms a sort of protecting shield to the young extremity of the root. Roots increase in diameter in the same manner as stems.

Roots are covered externally by a modified epidermis —that is, by one or more layers of flattened tabular cells, but without stomates; this is also furnished with hair-like prolongations, which are commonly termed *fibrils.*

Internal Structure.—In *exogenous plants* the root in its internal structure resembles the stem, except that it has commonly no pith or medullary sheath; hence the fibro-vascular system here forms a central axis. In *endogenous plants* the internal structure of the root corresponds in every particular to that of the stem; and the same is the case with the roots of *acrogenous plants.*

QUESTIONS.

1. In what respects does the root resemble the stem?
2. How do roots grow in length?
3. How do roots increase in diameter?
4. What is the nature of the covering of roots?
5. What are fibrils?
6. What are the peculiarities of structure between exogenous stems and roots?
7. Do the roots of endogenous and acrogenous plants present any differences of structure from the stems of such plants?

SECTION III.—OF THE LEAF.

Leaves, with reference to their structure, are divided into *aerial* and *submerged*. By the former we mean those that live entirely or partially in the air, and by the latter those that, dwell wholly immersed in water.

1. *Aerial Leaves.*—The simplest leaves, as those of Mosses, are formed simply of cellular tissue; but in plants above these they consist of both a cellular and fibro-vascular system, the latter of which is in direct connection with that of the stem or branch. The cellular system constitutes the soft parts of the leaf, and the fibro-vascular system the hard parts, which, by their ramification, form the veins. The whole is clothed by the epidermis, which is furnished with stomates, hairs, and glands, in the manner already described (pages 110 and 111).

In most leaves the fibro-vascular system is double, and in dicotyledonous plants the upper layer is then in connection with, and corresponds in structure to, the wood, and the lower layer is continuous with the liber or inner bark, with which it also agrees in structure. This double layer may be readily seen in what are called *skeleton leaves*, or those in which the cellular tissue between the veins has been destroyed by maceration in water or by some other means. The leaves lying in a damp ditch in the winter months will afford good illustrations of such leaves, or they may be artificially prepared by maceration in acidulated water and in other ways.

The cellular tissue surrounds the veins (fig. 134, *fv*), and is placed between the epidermis of the upper and lower surfaces of the leaf. The cells, *ps*, beneath the epidermis, *es*, of the upper surface of the leaf are commonly closely compacted, and have but few or any intervals between them; but the cells, *pi*, below the epidermis, *ei*, of the under surface of the leaf are loosely arranged, and have numerous interspaces (fig. 134, *l*). This difference in the arrangement of the cells beneath the two surfaces of leaves arises from the fact that stomates are more abundant on the epidermis of their under surface, and have corresponding inter-spaces in the cellular tissue beneath, by which a free communication between the interior of the leaf and the external air, which is essential to the due performance of its functions is maintained.

Fig. 134.

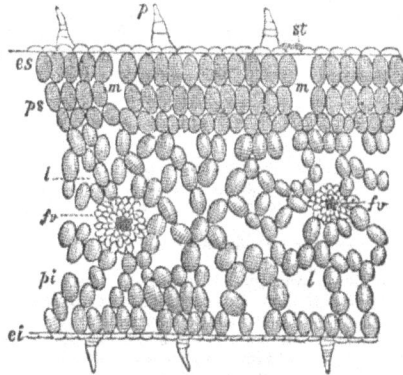

Fig. 134.—Highly magnified vertical section of the leaf of a Melon: *es*, epidermal tissue of the upper surface, furnished with hairs, *p*, and sto-mates, *st* ; *ei*, epidermal tissue of the lower surface : *ps*, three layers of cells beneath upper surface ; *pi*, cells beneath lower surface : *fv*, veins ; *m*, cavi-ties connected with the stomates ; *l*, cavities be-tween the loose cellular tissue of the under surfaces.

In the floating leaves of aquatic plants, as the stomates must be placed in direct communication with the air, they are most abundant on the upper surface, and the loose cellular tissue is then beneath them, and the compactly-arranged cells near the under surface—the position of parts being here, therefore, completely reversed.

2. *Submerged Leaves.*—In such leaves we have no fibro-vascular tissue, and no epidermis furnished with stomates, but the whole leaf is made up of cellular tissue, except when much thickened, and then such leaves have large air-cavities (page 112), by which their specific gravity is diminished, and they are thus readily suspended in the water.

With the leaf we finish the description of the internal structure of all the organs which are necessary to the life of the plant, and as all the organs which succeed the leaf are constructed of the same elements, simply modified to adapt them to the peculiar functions they have to perform, their special description would involve much repetition, and is unnecessary in such an elementary work as the present.

QUESTIONS.

1. What is meant by aerial and submerged leaves?
2. What is the structure of the leaf of a Moss?
3. What structures are found in the leaves of plants above Mosses?
4. Describe the fibro-vascular system of an aerial leaf in an exogenous plant.
5. What are skeleton leaves, and how are they prepared?
6. Describe the arrangement of the cells beneath the epidermis of the upper and lower surfaces of a leaf.
7. What is the cause of this difference of arrangement in the cells of the upper and lower surfaces of a leaf?
8. What are the peculiarities of structure presented by the floating leaves of aquatic plants?
9. What are the distinctive peculiarities of structure between submerged and aerial leaves?
10. What is the use of the air-cavities in thick submerged leaves?

THE END.

LONDON:
PRINTED BY JAS. TRUSCOTT AND SON,
Suffolk Lane, City.